Furkids

&

Ferals

Clarissa Wolf

Avid Readers Publishing Group

Lakewood, California

Furkids & Ferals

Avid Readers Publishing Group

http://www.avidreaderspg.com

ISBN-13: 978-1-61286-100-5

Printed in the United States

Dedication

To all the cats; loved, forgotten, lost and abandoned.

Acknowledgements

To my late parents, Mike and Theresa, who never lectured, but guided us by their actions. They demonstrated hard work, integrity, and helping others.

To my siblings, Claudia, Lyndia and Myron for their support, encouragement and help with my feral cat activities.

To Dr. Dennis Boileau (DVM) for guiding me through the TNR process and to the entire staff of Chanhassen Veterinary Clinic for handling the cats that don't like to be touched.

To Minnesota Spay Neuter Assistance Program (MN SNAP), Blue Sky Veterinary Services, LLC for offering low cost spay and neuter services for all Minnesota free-roaming cats.

To Diane (Ganzer) Baum for starting me on the path to publishing my books and for her persistence in getting me to print these stories.

To Melanie Strei for her edits, comments and feedback.

Front Cover

Pictured are Klondike and Mr. Cranky Pants.
Their stories are included in this book.

Proceeds

All proceeds from the sale of this book benefit the
stray and feral cats of Minnesota.

It all started with one cat.

Forward

Why Do I Work with Feral Cats?

After several years of volunteering for local animal rescue agencies, I decided to go off on my own and work with feral cats. I enjoyed working with the rescues, but none of them had a feral cat program, so I started my own. After volunteering for years in animal rescue, I had no idea what a feral cat was until 2004 when I saw one cat repeatedly on my walks through the woods with my dog, Qwincy. That one cat changed my life and my personal mission.

I started Spay the Strays, Fix the Ferals in 2004 to practice Trap, Neuter, Return (TNR). TNR is an internationally recognized program to humanely reduce the number of feral cats. A feral cat is a domestic cat that has had no human contact, so they have returned to a wild state and view humans as a threat. In TNR, feral cats are humanely trapped, evaluated by a veterinarian, vaccinated, spayed/neutered and ear-tipped. Once the cat has recovered from the surgery, they are returned to their home territory and a cat caretaker ensures they have food, water and shelter. The eartip shows that the cat has already been through the TNR process. There are often many cats of the same coloration in a colony, so the eartip easily identifies which have already been sterilized. If the cat cannot be returned to its home location for any reason, they are relocated to another colony. Friendly cats and kittens are put up for adoption.

Many people ask me why I decided to work with feral cats and some days I ask myself that same question. It isn't really a glamorous calling: I've been hissed at, spit on, scratched, bitten, sprayed, peed and pooped on. I have to get unwilling cats out of traps, into crates, then into carriers to go to the veterinarian then back into a crate, all while the cats are doing the aforementioned things to me. I have to provide them food, water and a clean litter box at the same time they are trying to get out of the crate. I'm constantly cleaning crates, litter boxes, food and water bowls and washing towels with bleach. Then why do I keep doing it? Really, who else would? Most everyone is willing to help a kitten or puppy in need, but few people want to deal with the nasty cats. I'm not blaming anyone for not helping the feral cats, it is a tough job, but I guess it is my calling. I used to ask what my purpose was in life and now I know I'm here for the feral cats.

The feral cats have taken me out of my comfort zone in so many ways. I love my solitude, so interacting with large groups of people, talking to people about feral cats, and participating in fundraising activities exhausts me. It is not something I would do for myself, but I do it for the ferals.

I feed two colonies of feral cats every day, no matter the temperature, rain or snow conditions or if I'm not feeling well. If I'm ever tempted to skip a day when it's freezing cold or I'm sick in bed, I just think of the feral cats that come running when I drive up to feed them. I know that they will sit there and wait for me all night and I can't disappoint them. I have never had to go to bed hungry, so they shouldn't have to either.

People often ask me if it wouldn't be better just to euthanize the feral cats when they are trapped, but I tell those people that every single feral cat I've trapped has proven to me they value their life. They growl and hiss, bite and scratch, and flail themselves against trap and crate with the desire to get out. If that isn't the will to live then I don't know what is. It's not the feral cats' fault that they live on the edge of society. Unfortunately, too many cats are lost or abandoned to survive on their own. They have no choice but to follow nature so they breed repeatedly. They cannot help themselves, so we need to help them.

I have been asked on several occasions if it is really worth the trouble? Am I making an impact? I may not be able to spay/neuter every feral cat, but at least the ones I have sterilized no longer have to worry about endlessly raising kittens, searching for food and fighting for territory. Also I have a voice and I can educate others in the plight of the feral cat. Part of that voice is writing books, not for financial gain as the money is donated to the feral cats, but to educate others.

I don't have special skills or knowledge. I learned everything on the fly, from other people, the internet, books, and trial and error. The cats aren't naturally drawn to me and I don't have a special connection to animals like some people do. I just have the willingness and determination to deal with nasty cats in order to provide them with a better life. I am very empathetic, but not by choice, it is just a part of me. I can put myself into the feral cat's furry little paws and feel the fear, the hunger and the exhaustion. It makes me want to cry, but that solves nothing. The only way I can make it better, is by helping them stop the cycle of breeding and ensure their basic needs of food, water and shelter are met. I hope with all of that, they don't just exist, but have the opportunity to enjoy life. When I feed the colonies I see them sitting in the sun, grooming each other, and getting excited knowing it is feeding time. It makes me smile because they are acting just like my indoor cats and that is a good life.

After seven years, 490 cats, and using much of my own finances, I changed the purpose of Spay the Strays, Fix the Ferals. I am not the type of person that can organize and lead a group of people to a purpose, so I did most everything on my own, from trapping to fundraising. It is a lot of work for one person. We are still a nonprofit raising money to maintain our current colonies of feral cats. I still trap feral cats but now I do it as a volunteer with Minnesota Spay Neuter Assistance Program (MN SNAP) and their TNR efforts. Of course, if I have room, I can never say no to pregnant ferals or feral mommas with kittens.

Several of the feral kittens I have trapped live with me now as part of my furry family. I kept them for a variety of reasons which are detailed in their stories in this book. I tend to keep the ones that are not considered adoptable due to issues with personalities, medical issues and head trauma. No matter their foibles, they are my furkids for the remainder of their lives. They enrich my life more than I could ever enrich theirs.

I hope the stories in this book demonstrate to you, as they do to me, that feral cats are worth the trouble. TNR is such a benefit to the feral cats and the community. The feral cats have longer, better lives and there are fewer of them wandering the streets of our neighborhoods. I know not everyone will have the same passion or see the feral cats as I do, but if just one story touches one heart, I hope that person will help educate others on their plight and support TNR in their community.

At the printing of this book, we have trapped/taken in a total of 521 stray and feral cats/kittens since 2004. I have listed the breakdown below:

Trapped:	521
Adopted:	242
Released:	227
*Euthanized:	31
**Died in Captivity:	17
Rehomed:	4

*Friendly cats/kittens are only euthanized if they are gravely ill. Feral cats are euthanized if gravely ill or if they test positive for feline leukemia since they will infect other cats if released.

**Along with other newborn kittens over the years, we had two full litters of kittens born to feral mothers that died soon after birth in 2011.

Introduction

For as long as I can remember, I wanted a cat or dog. Growing up in Bismarck, ND, my mom only allowed us to have fish, hamsters and rabbits as pets because she felt that dogs and cats belonged outside.

When I was nine years old my desire to have a cat or dog as a pet was so strong, that when a neighbor watched her son's cat while he was on vacation, I pretended the cat was mine. The cat was kept outside because the neighbor didn't want anything to do with cat sitting so when the cat would come over to our yard seeking attention, I happily obliged. I bought her cat food and treats and when I would lie on the grass in the backyard, the cat would curl up on my stomach. I was in heaven. Of course, our relationship was fleeting because the owner came back from vacation and the cat went home.

It was almost 20 years later that I adopted my first cat while in the United States Air Force stationed at Osan Air Force Base in South Korea. At the time I was married to another airman and we lived off base in a Korean apartment building. A co-worker of mine had recently taken in a stray cat that promptly had kittens and my husband and I adopted two of them. We named the kittens Streak, an orange tabby that streaked across the floor, and Scamp, a calico that scampered along after Streak.

At the time a spay was considered an elective surgery and the military veterinarians' main priority was caring for the police dogs so we went on a waiting list to have Streak and Scamp spayed. In the meantime the kittens went into heat several times. I still remember the days and nights of incessant howling and I was so glad when it was finally our turn to have them spayed. We had to take them to the base in Seoul, so Streak and Scamp had to ride on the bus as our military rank didn't qualify to own a car. We had to buy a ticket for them to occupy a seat and luckily they were relatively quiet on the bus ride.

When we were transferred back to the U.S. Streak and Scamp made the long airplane ride with us from Korea. When my husband and I later divorced, Streak and Scamp traveled with me to Minneapolis, MN. With another airplane ride under their furry belts, I promised them no more flights, they were earth bound now. For everything they went through in traveling by bus, airplane and car, they were the best cats. They never held a grudge after all I put them through. Scamp died at the age of 10 due to a heart condition and Streak died at the age of 15. Streak became so despondent after Scamp passed away, that I adopted another cat, Izzabelle, to hopefully get her interested in life again. Izzabelle is a beautiful silver tabby exotic shorthair, which is basically a Persian mix. She has the short face, but the fur is not as long as a Persian's. She was surrendered due to scratching the children in the household, which baffled me, since they had declawed her. Since Izzy was used to other cats and dogs, she was the perfect candidate to join the family. Eventually, Streak came out of her funk and went on to accept Izzy as a companion.

Though I had a late start in life with cat guardianship, I have definitely made up for it since then with over 500 hundred cats and kittens parading through my life. I hope you enjoy reading the stories as much as I enjoyed living them.

The Love of my Life
Qwincy

I bought Qwincy, a Papillon, from a breeder when he was an eight-week-old puppy (Yes, my cats are all rescues, but my dog is a pure bred). I had done a lot of research on dogs and determined a Papillon was the best fit not just because of size and personality, but for their adaptability to travel. Qwincy was just ten weeks old when he took his first six hour car ride to visit my dad in Bismarck. At twelve weeks, he took his first airplane flight in a carrier under the seat in front of me on another trip to Bismarck. Over the years, he's taken many trips to visit my dad by car and airplane and he was always the perfect traveler. My dad has since passed and Qwincy now takes shorter trips by car to visit family, but he is still an excellent travel companion.

My dad loved Qwincy and spoiled him rotten. I would glimpse my dad sneaking Qwincy tidbits under the table at mealtime and he loved the way Qwincy would tear up newspaper inserts, so he indulged Qwincy in this passion.

Qwincy is larger than the breed standard for a Papillon, which is something I'm actually grateful for. He isn't as delicate as most Papillons, so I don't have to worry about thin legs breaking easily. This came in handy when we did agility activities for awhile, but sadly Qwincy was diagnosed with a luxating patella we had to quit that activity. Now we walk for miles and hours when the weather cooperates and he loves our visits to the dog park.

Qwincy is quite the barker, but there are some occasions when he should have barked, but didn't. Once my sister's cat had him cornered in the bathroom and another time I accidently locked him in the laundry room. On both occasions I couldn't find him and called his name, but he didn't make a peep.

Because Qwincy was raised with my cats, he thinks he is a cat. Even though he is socialized well with other dogs and has gone to doggy daycare since he was four months old, he can climb the cat tower (albeit not as gracefully as a cat). This feline-like prowess has made him the perfect partner in taming countless feral kittens over the years. The kittens tend to warm up to Qwincy first, and when they see him interacting with me they learn the human is okay.

I always tell Qwincy he has to live to be at least twenty years old, even though the breed standard is fifteen years. He is ten years old as I write this book and I can't imagine my life without him. He barks far too much and does naughty things just to see if I'm paying attention, but he is the love of my life.

Specs
The Feral Cat that Started it All

After living in Chaska, MN for several years my dog Qwincy and I started seeing more and more stray cats on our daily walks through the woods across the street from my home. Throughout the years there had always been a cat or two, but in the summer of 2004 the cat population increased dramatically. I knew something had to be done for these homeless cats, but I didn't know what.

After seeing the same beautiful Siamese mix cat for three days in a row, I decided it was time to do something. I went to the local hardware store and purchased a raccoon-sized live trap and baited it with a can of moist cat food. Within 15 minutes I trapped the cat I had seen for the previous three days. Great, now I had the cat, but I had absolutely no idea what to do next. I started by naming her Specs because the markings around her eyes made it look like she was wearing glasses. Then, I set up a litter box and food/water bowls in my downstairs bathroom and gave her the run of the room. Mostly she stayed behind the toilet.

At the time I thought I could tame this feral cat. However, after many hours of sitting in the downstairs bathroom reading to her, talking to her, and bribing her with every tasty morsel I could think of, it wasn't happening. Later, I read about the difficulty of taming feral cats, but at the time I thought I could work some sort of magic. It turns out I'm no cat whisperer.

Of course trying to catch her in the bathroom to take her to the veterinarian was a feat, but by using a towel I finally got her into a crate. I took Specs to her veterinary appointment and the vet determined that Specs was about a year old and had at least one litter of kittens before I trapped her.

Once Specs was all checked out, I explained what I had done and about my desire to help the many stray cats around my neighborhood, but confessed that I didn't know what to do. Then the vet described the Trap Neuter Return (TNR) process, where feral cats are trapped, evaluated, vaccinated and spayed/ neutered by a veterinarian, then released back and provided food, water and shelter by a cat caretaker. After reading more about the TNR process online, I realized that after volunteering with animal rescue groups for years, I had never heard of a feral cat and I had no idea what their plight was. Obviously if I didn't know about feral cats, then the majority of society likely had no idea either. I believe everything happens for a reason and Specs sat in that same location for three days straight waiting for me to notice and do something. It took awhile for me to take her hint, but I decided it was time I became an advocate for this forgotten and unknown type of cat.

After Specs was vetted and spayed, I returned her to the wooded area and set up my first feral cat feeding station. Because there were still several cats in the wooded area, I trapped them also and a few weeks later I applied to be a nonprofit organization, and

Spay the Strays, Fix the Ferals was born in August 2004. I was hoping to put myself out of business in two years, but seven years later I was still trapping feral cats.

Ivan the Feral
...or Mad Cat Rodeo!
Previously Published in the *Chaska Herald*

When I initially started Spay the Strays, Fix the Ferals, I let the feral cats have the run of my downstairs bathroom (one at a time), but I quickly learned to keep the ferals in crates for easier handling.

For every sport, the participants wear the appropriate attire. For catching feral cats in the basement bathroom to take them to the veterinarian, I wore a long-sleeved shirt, thick leather gloves and carried a couple of old towels. I would find where the cat was hiding in the bathroom, throw a towel over it, pick up the towel-covered cat, put it in the carrier and shut the door. If I was lucky, the cat would be hiding in the empty trash can so I could put the towel over the top of the garbage can, pick it up, turn it upside down over the crate, drop it in and close the carrier door. Voilá!

Then there was Ivan, the feral. Ivan was a large, beautiful Siamese mix I trapped in a wooded area. Ivan hid at first in my downstairs bathroom, but when the towel went over him, he sprang into action. Ivan spent a lot of time airborne, flying about the room and when he did land, it was on top of the shower stall. After watching his acrobatic performance for a while, I finally decided I needed more cat-catching equipment. Hoping that my brother kept a fishing net in the boat he stored at my house, I went out to the garage. Uncovering the boat, there it was. Success! A fishing net! There was even a bonus, the net was made of rubber and more durable than other fishing nets I had seen.

I went back into the bathroom armed with the net and Ivan was still on top of the shower stall. I made a swipe with the net, and missed, so he went airborne again. After some time and more acrobatic feats, I finally trapped him under the net when he landed on a flat surface. Then Ivan and I both took the opportunity to rest and catch our breath for a few minutes. I placed the towels over the top of the net and though it was still a struggle, I finally got Ivan into the carrier and quickly closed the door. After the 20 minute rodeo, I had worked up quite a sweat, but amazingly I didn't get scratched or bitten, so it had a good outcome and I counted it as my aerobic workout for the day.

Ivan was finally vaccinated, neutered and back in the basement bathroom. I wasn't looking forward to his release date, since I would have to participate in another "Mad Cat Rodeo"!

Gulliver and Smudge
The First Feral Kittens

Gulliver and Smudge were my first feral kittens and were about six weeks old when they were trapped. They had been living under a mobile trailer home and the resident said she hadn't seen their mother in three or four days. The kittens ate the canned cat food in the trap hungrily, so at least they were weaned.

I left the feral kittens alone for a couple of days in a cat condo crate in my downstairs craft room so they could settle down and get used to household activity and noises. After a few days I started trying to tame them by petting them with a fake hand I fashioned out of a garden glove and a small wooden handle. However, Gulliver and Smudge weren't too thrilled with it and kept hissing at me.

I did some reading online on taming feral kittens and they recommended feeding them chicken baby food using a spoon so they associate the hand with good things. I didn't have baby food handy, so I tried moist cat food and that worked wonders. Smudge, the black kitten, took to it right away but the orange tabby, Gulliver, took more convincing. She did finally eat the moist cat food, but hissed each time my hand started towards her. It made me laugh. Towards the end, she stopped the hissing and just ate. After they finished with the moist cat food, they actually started playing, the first time since they had been trapped. The information I read said that with kittens eight weeks and older it can take two to four weeks to tame them, but I was hoping it would go quicker. They were good about using the litter box, so that was one hurdle done.

After a few days, Smudge let me pet him whenever I wanted to, but Gulliver still hissed unless there was moist food on a spoon in front of her face. They were adorable and I loved to watch them play.

Gulliver and Smudge weren't thrilled with being handled. At their first veterinarian checkup, Gulliver did bite the vet, but she said it is her fault since she wasn't paying attention when it happened. Both kittens were healthy, except for a few worms which they were treated for with medicine. The vet estimated that they were eight weeks old, so I was correct in thinking they were probably about six weeks old when I trapped them. I was still spoon-feeding them moist food twice a day and they started to even come part of the way out of the crate to eat.

After another week, the kittens finally started to play outside the condo crate. On their first outing, after I finished spoon-feeding them, I left the crate door open and they stayed out and played. I blocked off an area to keep them contained in one corner of the craft room, but little Smudge was all over the basement. I called him Hot Shot, because he seemed like a brave little lion after being timid for so long. Much to his surprise, Qwincy came downstairs when Smudge was still out of the 'secure' area. Qwincy was happy to play, but Smudge wasn't impressed. I had never seen a kitten get so puffed up. He was a true "Halloween" cat, black, arched back and puffed out tail. It made me laugh. I moved Qwincy away long enough for Smudge to get back into the blocked off area and the kittens calmed down. It was an exciting night for everyone.

I named Gulliver correctly, even though she was actually a girl. Two nights after they first played outside the condo crate, it was "Gulliver's Travels" night. After I spoon-fed the kittens, I left the crate door open so they could play outside the condo crate again. Smudge was his adventurous self, exploring all over the basement. Gulliver watched from the area I blocked off. Eventually, Gulliver ventured out too and then decided to run upstairs. I thought she would come back down right away, but after about 15 minutes I went looking for her. I searched the house and finally found her under the couch. In trying to coax her out, she ran and I thought she returned downstairs. Well, she didn't. I didn't think of closing the doors to the bedrooms while she was under the couch, so I had to search the whole house again. I finally found her under my bed and was able to catch her with a small net. Too adventurous for me, we were both tired after all that fun.

Smudge became used to Qwincy finally and they would chase each other around the basement and played well together. However, Gulliver wouldn't venture far from the confined area after her adventurous trip upstairs.

On the second trip to the veterinarian, the veterinarian thought they may be from different litters because Smudge had adult teeth coming in already, which made him at least four months old and

Gulliver still had all baby teeth, so she was younger than Smudge. They did keep Smudge overnight to neuter him, but the vet wanted to wait until Gulliver was closer to four months before she was spayed. I picked up Smudge after work on the day he was neutered and he was very active for having surgery. That day I also learned that female feral kittens take longer to become tame compared to male feral kittens, which explained why Smudge was so much friendlier than Gulliver. I found that very interesting and also reassuring, since I thought I was doing something wrong with Gulliver.

Smudge worked on me for awhile, trying to convince me to keep him as one of my furkids. He would follow me around, and when I finally had the opportunity to sit on the couch for awhile, he would head greet me, curl up on my shoulder and purr in my ear. Cats in a family or colony rub their heads against each other as they pass and this is referred to as head greeting. Cats have glands on the side of their faces and by rubbing together they are sharing their scent to reinforce their bond. Cats will do the same to humans and dogs in the family and it is a sign of acceptance into the cat family. It is not always targeted to the head. If the cat cannot reach their human's face, they will rub up against legs as well. Smudge even started greeting Qwincy enthusiastically and they played well together. Smudge and Gulliver didn't spend a lot of time together anymore, Smudge hung out with Qwincy and me and Gulliver hung out with the new kitten, Shade. When it was time, they both went up for adoption and found great homes.

I had survived taming my first feral kittens. It was definitely a learning experience and was a great base to start in taming countless feral kittens in the future.

People often tell me they would never be able to give up a kitten after having it in their home for so long but once they are ready to be adopted out, I am usually happy to see them go. It is a lot of work to tame feral kittens. They are not the cute little balls of fur most people see on TV or at an adoption event. Feral kittens are hissing, spitting little whirlwinds with very sharp claws and teeth. They have never had human contact, so to them, a human is just as dangerous as a dog, or a bird of prey. They do not trust those that are trying to improve their lives so it takes hours of time, energy and dedication to get them tame enough to be a family pet. Yes, in the end it is worth it, but in the moment it can be discouraging and draining.

Shade
Abandoned in a Box

Every spring and summer I spend my time taming feral kittens. A volunteer from a local animal rescue agency came home from work one afternoon and found a box on her porch. The box had holes cut in it and in marker was written "Danger." Inside the box was a tiny feral kitten and someone had just dumped it at her home with no explanation. She called me to ask if I could take the kitten so I went and picked it up. The kitten was tiny, smaller than Smudge and Gulliver when I had trapped them, so it was probably about five weeks old. It was able to eat moist cat food, so at least it was weaned and was a pretty gray tabby I named Shade. The kitten was terrified, so I left it alone for a couple of days before I started to tame her.

After a week, Shade went to the veterinarian and received her first vaccinations. I moved her out of the downstairs bathroom into the craft room with Smudge and Gulliver. Smudge and Gulliver were in a cat condo crate, which was about four and a half feet high and Shade was in a smaller crate on top of the condo crate. She was still too little to go in with the 'big' kitties, so she had a spot all her own where she could watch Smudge and Gulliver play. When I started spoon-feeding Shade she didn't just hiss, she growled too. It was cute and I kept telling her that I wasn't afraid. When she actually started playing with the toys I had in her crate I knew she was feeling more comfortable.

One day while Smudge and Gulliver were out playing, Gulliver climbed up the outside of the condo crate like it was a ladder got on top of Shade's crate and then started playing with Shade through the bars. I didn't want to spoil the moment, so I didn't even try to go for the camera.

As soon as Shade was done being treated for internal parasites, she was able to get out of her crate to play with the bigger kittens. When I first let Shade out, they all played so well together. Shade was about half the size of the bigger kittens and she usually ended up at the bottom of the pile, but she was spunky and gave the bigger kittens a run for their money. I still kept Shade in her own crate at night, so she had a chance to eat and rest from the bigger kittens pestering her.

Even though she played well with the other kittens, Shade was still a nasty little thing towards people and she definitely didn't like Qwincy. So, I started to look for a location where she could be released or become a barn cat. Shade must have heard what was going on in my head because one day when she was out playing, she came up to me, started rubbing against my leg and meowed up at me for attention. From then on, humans were good and she was able to go up for adoption.

Later, I talked to the volunteer who I got Shade from and she had finally found out who left the kitten on her doorstep. It was a friend of a relative who stopped in Minneapolis and heard meowing from his engine. When he looked there was Shade in the engine. I don't remember where he started out from, but I'm sure it wasn't a pleasant ride for the kitten no matter how far the truck traveled.

Dodger

Dodger was a very pretty cat, white with black markings including a black stripe down his nose. However, Dodger wasn't so happy about captivity. After letting him relax for a few hours after he was trapped, I went into the feral cat room (my downstairs bathroom) to take his picture for the website and he freaked out, trying to climb out of the back of the crate. Poor guy.

I'm not going to sugar coat it: Dodger was the Cat from Hell! Like playing the children's game and trying to dodge the ball, Dodger was not about to stay still and get caught. Outside of Ivan, the Feral, it usually takes me about two minutes to get a feral cat out of the crate and into a cat carrier to go to the veterinarian. The morning I took Dodger to the vet, it took me 30 minutes to get him out. I was sweating profusely by the time I was done. I thought about just loading the entire crate into the truck, but then the vet would have had to try to get him out and they probably would have charged me double for that. They may have been able to stick a needle into him while in the crate to knock him out and remove him, but the crate is more spacious than a carrier, so I didn't want to risk my luck. I was late to work for a meeting with my supervisor that morning because of Dodger. I guess I named him right.

After neutering, male cats can be released immediately, but I usually keep the male cats for 24 hours after they are neutered. I made an exception on Dodger's part because I didn't want to spend another 30 minutes trying to get him out of the crate in order to release him. I kept him in the cat carrier overnight and released him in the morning on my way to work.

Pewter
Really a Tank

Pewter was a huge gray tabby tomcat that seemed to be a very mellow cat. He wasn't bothered by me adding food and water to his dishes in his crate or switching out litter boxes. He seemed so laid back, I was even thinking about trying out the fake hand on him to see if he could be petted. I use the fake hand (stuffed garden glove on a thick stick) to test if cats are friendly without risking my own hand.

Yes, Pewter was mellow...until I touched him! He became monster wild cat when I tried to get him out of the crate on the day he had to go to the veterinarian. I just put the towel over him, started to pick him up and he went into action. I think he was saving up all week for that morning. He was a huge, very thick and sturdy cat that I should have named Tank. It was tough keeping a hold on him, but I did finally get him into the cat carrier without being scratched or bitten. He did rip a few holes in the towel, so I was lucky I was left unscathed.

When I prepared to release Pewter after he recovered from his neuter, trying to catch him to release him was awful. He wasn't going to let me get a hold of him a second time, even with the net. I finally resigned myself to loading the entire crate into the truck. A little cumbersome and awkward, but it got the job done. When I got to the release site and opened the door of the crate, he was gone in a gray flash.

Pewter held no grudges though. He would always show up for feeding time the minute I stepped out of the truck. He kept his distance, but he never missed a meal.

Lucifur

Sometimes it is difficult to determine the gender of a feral cat at first glance. Lucifur was all black, but with his broad nose and wide jowls, I was sure it was a male. I called him Lucifur because he was the nastiest cat I had trapped yet. Lucifur would go right for the face every chance he got. In addition, once I got him into his crate, he somehow removed his water dish from the bars of the crate (it was attached with a bolt mind you) and soaked everything in sight. I couldn't let him sit in water until he went to the veterinarian so I had to move him to a dry crate. I wasn't looking forward to catching him even once, and now I had to catch him at least twice. I'm pretty sure I was paying for something bad I did in my youth.

At the time the local Veterinarian Technical School spayed and neutered some feral cats for me free, so when I took Lucifur in for his vaccinations and neuter, I was very detailed in how nasty he was to handle. I had put a large red note on his carrier with "Caution" written in large black letters. I moved him from the carrier to their holding crate myself, and put another red Caution note there as well.

When the school director called me later to say everything went well with the neuter, she mentioned that Lucifur had bitten a student. I had warned them repeatedly about him and labeled the crate, but the director said it was the student's fault. The student had sat in front of Lucifur's crate and petted him despite the warnings. Now I had to hold the nasty cat for 10 additional days to ensure he didn't have rabies. The director recommended that I get a rabies vaccination too, because I deal with feral cats, so at least one good thing came out of it.

Lucifur continued to be an unruly guest during his additional 10 day stay, but he was finally released and exited the crate without a backward glance.

Cuddles
Caregivers and their Ferals

If there ever was a misnomer for a cat, it was for a pregnant feral cat named Cuddles. Cuddles was a beautiful, black, pregnant cat someone had been feeding in their yard and this cat had an attitude.

Most of the pregnant feral cats I've had in my home had their kittens during the night and Cuddles was no different. But when I checked on her in the morning, there was only one kitten, which is extremely unusual. Momma cats will sometimes eat deceased kittens so I'm not sure how many kittens she actually had.

Once I moved Cuddles and her kitten, Puzzle, out to the craft room where I had the condo crates, I couldn't wait to get the nasty momma cat out of my house. I found it ironic that the caretaker had named her Cuddles! Cuddly she wasn't! One day, Cuddles got out of the condo crate in the craft room and she spread excrement as she ran and hid under a craft table. It was a long and nasty cleanup process to remove the traces she left.

Puzzle was adorable and loved playing with Qwincy. I do feel a little guilty about putting the kittens up for adoption, because Qwincy plays with them so well, but I have to think of my sanity. I'm used to my older cats that don't climb curtains, knock items off counters/tables and steal the ribbon bookmarks out of my books. Kittens are cute, but so naughty. It's adorable the way Qwincy played with Puzzle though. Because she was so tiny, Qwincy would lie down on the floor to play with her and they were so cute together.

I was very happy and relieved the day I was able to release Cuddles back to her home territory and I'm sure she was equally happy to be out of my house.

Lucy
Surrogate Mom

Lucy was a pretty white and brown tabby cat who looked like she was already ear-tipped, since her ears were rugged and short. As part of the TNR process, when feral cats are spayed/neutered, they are also ear-tipped. The veterinarian takes off the top quarter inch of the feral cat's left ear. Ear-tipping is an international recognized identification system to show that a feral cat has already been sterilized. The ear tip can be seen from a distance so any caretakers or animal control agents can determine that a cat is already sterilized without having to trap. If an ear-tipped cat does make it into a trap again, the ear tip is easily recognized and the cat can be released immediately.

Lucy was living on a farm with many feral cats, but for some reason she was the friendliest amongst the nastiest. She was pregnant when trapped and I had made a veterinarian appointment on a Friday to have her checked and get an approximate due date. I checked Lucy every night to see if she was dripping milk which indicates a delivery will happen soon. I checked her Wednesday and no dripping milk, so I was very surprised when I walked into the downstairs bathroom Thursday morning and Lucy was nursing three kittens. I still took her to the vet on Friday to have her ears checked and to have a feline leukemia test. Her feline leukemia test was negative and the only issue with her ears was frostbite.

A few days later another veterinarian contacted me to see if Lucy would accept four orphaned kittens. The kittens were found in a covered boat that had been taken out of storage, but the kittens weren't discovered until the boat was uncovered three days later. The kittens had been bottle fed over the weekend by a veterinary technician and I picked them up on Tuesday. I had brought along the cat bed that Lucy and her kittens had been sleeping on so the orphans would smell like their new family and increase their chances of Lucy adopting them. When I got home, I rubbed Lucy's kittens on the orphans to make sure they smelled right and put the kittens in with Lucy and her family. Lucy didn't bat an eye. She smelled each new kitten in turn, then went back to the first one and started cleaning them. Lucy treated the kittens like her own from the start.

When I checked on her later, there was a row of kittens sleeping in front of Lucy. I tried to bottle feed the new kittens formula to take some of the pressure off Lucy for having four additional mouths to feed. However, now that the kittens were back on real milk, they wouldn't take the formula. I made sure Lucy had as much to eat as she possibly could ingest and hoped she had enough milk for everyone since I had more than doubled her family.

Unfortunately one of the orphans, Evenrude had been injured by a dog before he came into my care. The dog had picked up Evenrude and injured his left rear leg when he was about 10 days old.

Once the other kittens became mobile, Evenrude was only able to scoot from place to place. I stared doing physical therapy with him twice a day to strengthen his back legs. He finally started using his left front foot and could hold his upper body up off the floor but he was still not able to walk like the other kittens. His right leg was fine, but the left leg got in the way when he tried to walk. With the physical therapy I was hoping that he would at least be able to use his right leg to get around if the left leg had to be amputated. He did reach milestones; he was finally able to play with the other kittens and he was able to stand on all four legs for short periods of time.

Unfortunately, I eventually had to euthanize poor little Evenrude. He was never able to walk on his back legs and he couldn't eliminate on his own, Momma cat and I had to help him with that function. Eventually his stomach became distended and rigid. One morning when I let the kittens out to play, Evenrude was unresponsive. He was still warm and he purred when I picked him up, but he wasn't fully awake. I took him to the vet the minute they opened and we determined it would be best to euthanize him. I was heartbroken. Evenrude tried so hard and I was planning on keeping him myself. It is amazing how much a little kitten can touch your heart in such a short period of time.

Sadie and Solo

I took in a pretty calico cat named Sadie from another organization. She had been in impound for two weeks and no one claimed her. She was very pregnant and less than 48 hours after I took her home, she had five kittens. Sadie was very emaciated and only one kitten survived. She was so skinny, I was surprised even the one kitten had lived. Sadie was a great mom. She was very protective of her kitten and would chase the other cats away when they got too close. She was also very affectionate and liked to be with people. When I sat at the computer desk, Sadie would sit behind me on the chair.

I named Sadie's only surviving kitten Solo. Solo was a gray and white tabby male who was very friendly and affectionate. He liked to snuggle in laps and lie on his back to have his tummy scratched. If the lap was covered with a book or laptop, Solo would just climb on top of the item and lay there instead. Solo loved to play with other cats, kittens and Qwincy. It took some time for Solo to understand that fingers weren't toys and should not be bitten.

I was so worried about Solo being the only kitten that survived because he wouldn't have a littermate to play with. However momma Sadie was so great about playing with him. Momma and son would go up and down the cat tower chasing each other. If I didn't pay enough attention to Solo when I was sitting at the computer desk, he would just climb up my pants leg and sit in my lap.

When Sadie went in for her spay surgery, the veterinarian found that she had been declawed at some point. I just couldn't understand who would declaw a cat and not have her spayed. Generally, both surgeries are done at the same time. While a declawed cat cannot claw furniture, an unspayed cat goes through several heat cycles a year. A declawed cat has to stay indoors because it has no defenses outside without claws. At cat in heat is very loud and the heat cycle lasts for several days. Cats in heat are driven by hormones and they will attempt to get outside to meet up with the males that can smell and hear her. If the declawed cat in heat gets outside to mate, it is now very vulnerable because it has no claws to defend herself from any type of danger.

I never checked Sadie's nails because if I can see them hanging out of the paw when they are retracted, I clip them, but if I don't see them I don't worry about it. Also, she went up and down the cat tower chasing Solo, so I'm not sure how she accomplished that with no front claws.

After Solo was weaned, Sadie was spayed so no more kittens and she would never have to be outside and clawless again. Both Sadie and Solo went up for adoption and found wonderful forever homes.

Beacon

I named him Beacon because he was solid black with a quarter-sized white spot in the middle of his chest. When I saw him in the woods, he blended in well with the darkness caused by the dense canopy of leaves, except for the white beacon on his chest. He was always there at feeding time, following me to the food dishes, but not getting too close. I got the impression that he was judging me somehow. I'm not sure how I measured up, but it probably wasn't good by the disapproving scowl on his face. Sometime after he was neutered and released, Beacon stopped showing up at mealtime and I was actually missing those kitty glares. It's always difficult not knowing what happens to the feral cats. Some of them stay around for years and others disappear, or they move on. Beacon had actually moved on.

Sometime later, I received a call from a resident about a feral cat she was feeding. It took a very long time to trap him, but finally we prevailed. I took him home and set him up in a crate, waiting to make an appointment with the veterinarian. Then I got a good look at him and realized he was already ear-tipped. I usually check while they are in the trap, but because I hadn't trapped in that location before, I hadn't bothered to check. Once I compared him to the pictures of previously trapped ferals, I realized it was Beacon. He had made his way out of the woods, between two businesses, across a busy highway, over the railroad tracks and then crossed another busy street and ended up at the resident's home. It was quite a trek for a cat that no longer had any testosterone urging him to find females and who had a ready supply of food and water. It did make sense why it was so difficult to trap him the second time because he knew what was coming. I did take Beacon back to the vet to get his vaccinations updated because it had been a year since he was first trapped.

Beacon did quite well for himself at his new location. He had a heated cat bed, a dogloo, a heated water dish and the resident fed him very high quality food.

Beacon stayed at his new location for some time, but he eventually moved on again.

The Trouble with Ice

It all started on a Saturday. Qwincy began barking like crazy at the sliding glass door downstairs. When I looked out I saw a gray cat that I had never seen before walking across the apartment parking lot behind my townhouse. Two white kittens were following her, single file, tails straight in the air. They crossed the street and entered the woods behind the dumpster by the rental townhomes. I kept watch to see if the mother cat and kittens walked by again, but they didn't.

Later Saturday, I checked the woods and the kittens were playing on a pile of dead grass about 30 feet from the street. The mother cat was nearby too, glaring at me. One of the townhouse residents was outside with her daughter so I asked if they knew if anyone was feeding the cat and kittens. She said no, but they had seen them around for some time. The resident said that kids had caught one of the kittens, and then let it go. I gave the resident my cell phone number and Spay the Strays, Fix the Ferals literature.

I set two traps Sunday and I checked them every half hour but it took a long time until I trapped anyone. I finally trapped one of the kittens, Frost, and later the mom, Misty. I continued trying to trap the second kitten, Ice and I even trapped into the night on Sunday, which I normally don't do, because after dark I usually only get raccoons and opossums. I got up every two hours to check the trap but unfortunately, all I caught was a big raccoon.

I tried trapping again Monday after work. I kept seeing the kitten in the same spot on the grass mound, but every time I got near, it took off. By Tuesday I was desperate, because I thought the kitten was too young to be away from its mom, and I was afraid it would starve. I decided to put the trap out all day Tuesday, even though I knew I wouldn't be able to check it until after work.

Tuesday morning, the momma cat and kitten went to the veterinarian. The vet called me later and said that Frost was at least eight weeks old and no longer nursing, so then I felt better about Ice still in the woods; at least it was weaned and not depending on momma's milk.

Momma cat was vaccinated and spayed. After work, I was on my way to the vet to pick up momma cat and kitten when my cell phone rang. It was the resident from the rental townhomes across the street. She said "The kitten is in the trap!" I was so relieved and happy. When I got to the woods, I looked under the towel covering the trap and I saw a white cat in the crate, but once I picked up the crate, I knew it couldn't be the kitten, it was too heavy. When I arrived home and got a better look, it was a white cat with the same one blue eye and one green eye as both kittens, but she was at least four months old and must have been from a previous litter.

I saw Ice again Wednesday morning before work, but I didn't leave the trap out because I knew I would be arriving home later from work that day. I didn't see Ice Wednesday night at all.

Thursday morning, I saw Ice again, and decided to leave the trap out all day again. I ran home at lunch to see if I had a kitten in the trap, but no luck.

That brings us to Friday. I saw Ice that morning again when Qwincy and I went out for our morning walk. I set the trap again. I wouldn't be able to run home at lunch to check the trap, but I was able to leave work early to check, but still no Ice in the trap.

Back at home, I brought Frost upstairs to bunk with Qwincy. I let him run around the basement when I was down there at night, but he seemed lonely and would cry once I all came upstairs to go to bed, so I brought him upstairs with us. Frost and Qwincy got along well. Frost followed Qwincy around like he was a momma cat and they played well together. Frost did like to play in water bowls though, so it was tough to keep enough water in his bowl for him to drink, but not too much or he flooded his crate.

Skipping ahead to Sunday, because I had no luck on Saturday, I set two traps and sat nearby. Ice came toward the traps and finally went inside one of them, but he didn't weigh enough to set off the trap. I went home and got a net and extra cans of cat food. Once Ice ate his fill, he moved off into the trees and started to groom himself with his back to me. I walked as slowly and quietly as I could. I was so desperate to get this kitten; I wasn't going to leave the area without him. I lowered the net over Ice and finally, I had the guy trapped.

After Ice had finally gone to the veterinarian for testing and vaccinations, it had been two weeks since Frost had been trapped and the difference between the two kittens was amazing. They were both white kittens with one green and one blue eye. However, Frost was nice and clean and had filled out. Ice was about half of Frost's size and he was filthy, he looked like a light gray kitten.

Frost went off to be adopted and I later received pictures from his new human mom and he is stretched out in her lap and loving all the attention.

I kept Ice longer because he was still a feral little thing. He would sit in my lap and play and allow me to pet him. Unfortunately, my father became ill during this time and I was back and forth to Bismarck so Ice didn't continue to receive much human social time, as he hid from the cat sitter.

When everything had settled down and I was back home, Ice was still very skittish and I decided to keep him. He wasn't adoptable, but he had been inside for so long, I didn't have the heart to release him outside once he was neutered.

I still have Ice. He is now a beautiful white sleek cat, one of the longest cats I have ever seen. He lets me pet him for short periods of time. It's a struggle to get his nails trimmed once a month, but I have the process down pat now and we get the front nails done without much incident. Ice gets along great with all of my cats and my dog, Qwincy.

After taking so long to trap Ice, I'm not about to let him out of my sight now, he is here to stay as an inside cat.

Dice
The Cat who Gave me Fleas

The first time I trapped Dice, he was probably about ten weeks old, on the cusp of the time he can be tamed. Unfortunately, there was a trap malfunction and Dice was able to slip out through a small gap in the trap's back door. I was devastated. I wanted to get him while he could still be tamed and become a loved indoor cat.

It was several weeks later when I finally trapped Dice again. At the veterinarian, they informed me he had fleas. I'm usually very diligent about keeping cats in the downstairs bathroom until the medication kills off the fleas, but I felt I had already lost valuable time with Dice, so I put him in the craft room in a condo crate.

Soon I was being driven to distraction by biting fleas. My furkids receive flea preventative, so the only thing the fleas had to lunch on was me. It was a miserable 36 hours until I could get a company at my house to spray for the fleas. I was so desperate; I considered putting dog flea preventative on my own neck to see if that would work. In the end, I wasn't brave enough to go that route. The only comfort I found was soaking in a tub of water. I had to explain to my boss that I had to work from home because I had fleas. Not embarrassing at all. I had to cancel a trip to the ceramic store with my sister because I was afraid of infecting anyone else with fleas.

Finally the exterminator came and sprayed for fleas and I finally felt relief.

I wasn't able to get Dice tamed and I was so disappointed, feeling I had failed him. If I had ensured the trap was secure the first time, he would have been young enough to tame and find a loving indoor home.

Dice is still in the same colony and even though I see him daily at feeding time, I still cringe with the memories of having fleas.

Jax
Cat 100

A resident in the local trailer court passed away and her family cleaned out the trailer and just let her two indoor-only cats loose outside to fend for themselves. Luckily, they were both friendly and could be adopted out after they had been to the veterinarian. I trapped the kitten, Jax and his older companion, Porter, the next day. Jax was the 100th cat trapped and I was very excited about breaking the 100 mark.

Little Jax was quite vocal. With his triangular face and vocalizations, I thought he must be part Siamese. One weekend when I had the windows open and his vocalizations were sounding like a baby crying, I figured the neighbors thought I was beating a child. I finally let Jax out of his crate and he had the run of the house. I knew it was a bit of a risk because he hadn't been tested for feline leukemia yet, but he was giving me a headache with his crying and my cats were vaccinated against feline leukemia, so I was willing to take the chance. With quality food, his black coat because soft and shiny.

Jax tested negative for feline leukemia, was vaccinated and neutered. He was a sweetheart and loved to follow me around the house and participate in what I was doing. He got along great with my cats and I was surprised how quickly they accepted him.

He still wasn't too sure about Qwincy, but didn't hiss at him much.

Then Jax, the six-month-old kitten who was abandoned outside after his owner passed away, landed the most incredible new home ever. My cat sitter/dog walker, adopted him. I was so excited because I get to cat sit Jax whenever his new mom goes on vacation. I get to see Jax several times a year now and he is a beautiful, well-loved cat.

Trinket
(aka) Little Trooper

I picked up two stray cats from animal control at the local reservation, one adult and one kitten, both buff tabbies. They were trapped during a cold snap in February. The kitten looked about eight weeks old and he was sneezing a lot. Luckily, I was able to get him into the veterinarian right away the next morning. The vet called me at work later that morning and told me the kitten was actually six months old. I was astonished. The vet said the kitten already had his adult teeth and due to lack of nutrition, he was small. The vet couldn't say if the kitten would ever get to full size. He was suffering from an upper respiratory infection, a belly full of two types of worms and ears severely infected by ear mites. Poor little guy. That is why I named him Little Trooper, because he has been through a lot, but he just kept going. Once on medication, the kitten quickly got better, but kept sneezing. I could tell he was feeling better because he was much more active and starting to be naughty.

Then I changed Little Trooper's name to Trinket. There was a mix up on her records and she was actually a girl, not a boy, so I felt compelled to give her a more girly name. I took her to the vet again and they said she was in good health, but may be sneezing from the dust in the cat litter or had an allergy. At the time, it was hard to find cat litter that wasn't dusty when scratched.

Trinket was great with all my cats and played with Qwincy. She purred the minute you touched her and loved to snuggle against a person's neck. She sat on shoulders for short periods of time and in laps for long periods of time.

Trinket went on to find her forever home. I'm not sure if she ever grew to be a full-sized cat.

Journey
(aka) Fluffy

Fluffy was surrendered by a family that had her as a barn cat and I took her in from another rescue agency. The rescue agency had her spayed and vaccinated, but Fluffy turned out to be rather wild and they couldn't tame her. The agency asked if I knew of a rescue that would take her. I told them I didn't, but I offered to put her in one of my feral cat colonies. The agency was hesitant about that option, but I was able to find a barn location that would take her. The barn was temperature controlled and the cats were provided food, water and litter boxes. The rescue agency liked the barn idea better, especially because Fluffy started out as a barn cat. The rescue agency took Fluffy to their veterinarian to have her boosters updated and I picked her up from there. While at the vet they found that she had two broken teeth and would need to have them extracted. The rescue agency didn't want to spend any more money on her because she wasn't adoptable, so I told them I would take care of the teeth.

My computer desk is downstairs in the same area as the cat condo crates and when I was on the computer one day, Fluffy started meowing for attention. I was surprised because adult feral cats don't meow. There are several different theories for why they don't meow; one is that it draws attention from predators and another is that cats communicate with

41

each other with a variety of sounds, but they only use meowing with humans. Since feral cats are not bonded to humans, they don't meow. After feeding feral cat colonies for several years, some of the cats do now meow when they see me, but I still cannot pet them. I just think they are telling me to "hurry up with the food already."

I opened the crate door and Fluffy let me pet and brush her. The next day she ventured a few steps out of the crate and ran back into it when she became startled by a noise. The following day, she ventured a few feet out of the crate and even walked up to my cat, Zander, touched noses with him and then head greeted him. Zander was probably more amazed than I was, he just sat there dazed. I hated to make her a barn cat now that she was interacting with me and the cats. She still wasn't too sure about Qwincy though. She was so sweet and pretty, but I wasn't sure how she would do with warming up to other people in order to become adoptable.

After Fluffy's teeth were pulled, she became the friendliest cat I have ever met in my life. She greets everyone that comes to the door and the minute they sit down, she is on their lap. It appears that the pain of the two broken teeth was causing her to be disagreeable. I decided that she had gone through enough already in her life, so I changed her name to Journey, and kept her as one of my furkids.

A Tale of Two Kitties

Cats aren't usually seen as social animals, but feral cats in a colony will pair up and have a companion to spend time with eating, grooming and lying in the sun.

Ajax is an orange tabby male feral cat that was trapped in a wooded area of Chaska and released back to the same location after he was neutered. He was all alone in the woods for some time, showing up for feeding time, but staying back until I walked far enough away that he felt comfortable eating.

Several months later, I had a male feral cat, Flame, also an orange tabby, who couldn't be released back to the location where he was trapped, so it was decided to release him in the same area as Ajax.

At feeding time, Flame usually ate first even though he was the new guy, then timid Ajax would eat after Flame left. After several months, Flame and Ajax were sitting next to each other eating from the same dish and were even seen grooming each other after feeding time.

Before these feral male cats were trapped and neutered, it is unlikely they would have become such close companions, because they would have been fighting for the rights to a female in heat. Now with hormones out of the equation, Ajax and Flame can enjoy each other's company and live out their lives with a friend.

Sassy
Cat Six Pack

I was taming two sets of feral kittens at once and hey all tamed up nicely except one. Sassy was about 16 weeks old when I trapped her. The optimum time to tame feral kittens is eight weeks, and it is more difficult at 12 weeks and at 16 weeks, not always successful. However, after the other kittens went up for adoption, I kept Sassy and hoped she would tame up. She would approach me when I had treats or moist food, but other than that, she hissed and ran to hide when I was near her. When it was finally time to have her spayed, she still wasn't tamed, but I had her inside for so long, I didn't have the heart to send her outside to live in a colony. Therefore, I had her spayed and she is now part of my furkid family.

Sassy recovered from her spay in a crate in my bedroom. She was still on some liquid medication to prevent infection, so I medicated her while she was crated by putting the meds in her moist food at night. The directions on one of the medications recommended it be administered under the cat's tongue. Hah! Even the receptionists at the vet's office said they would like a film clip of me trying to do that with Sassy.

Sassy was adorable when she played as a kitten. She was often "surprised" by her tail and had to chase it. She loved the other cats and tolerated Qwincy.

Adult feral cats usually never become friendly enough to be adoptable house cats. Some can be tamed, but it can take months or even years and then they will just bond to the one person that tamed them. If they are adopted out, they wouldn't bond to the new owner and would essentially be feral.

Sassy has been in my house for five years now and she still isn't tame. I can pet her once a day when I feed moist food, but just one pet, any more than that and she takes off. She has never meowed and I have never heard her purr.

She gets along with the other cats and tolerates Qwincy. I do catch her playing on occasion, so she seems happy enough with her lot in life.

Saving Sugar

A resident had several feral cats living on her property, including a momma cat with two kittens. One of the kittens was very sick and the resident was able to pick it up because it was too ill to run away.

I kept the momma cat, Chloe and the white kitten, Spice together for the first two nights. The first night, I don't think they moved. They didn't eat or drink, which is normal for feral cats and their first night of captivity. The second night, they trashed their crate. There was food, water and litter everywhere. I was able to get Spice out quickly to move him to the craft room to start his taming, but Chloe put up such a fight just to move her from her trashed crate to a new one. She was quite the fighter. I finally did get her to a clean crate. The next morning, her crate was trashed again, and I put off moving her to a clean crate until the caffeine started to work in my bloodstream.

Spice was very wild so I wasn't sure if she would tame up. I put her in with a tamed kitten, hoping she would learn to like humans. However, she bit me good one day, down to my knuckle, so it wasn't progressing as well as I hoped.

The other kitten, Sugar, was very ill with parasites that were sapping all her resources. She didn't like the medication, but she was so weak, it was easy to medicate her. She was such a little thing. I fed her kitten food and as much moist food as she could eat to hopefully get some weight on her. I could feel her backbone protruding when I pet her.

Kitten Spice had parasites too, but not to the extent that Sugar did. It was more of a challenge to medicate him daily. I did get both syringes in his mouth the first time but he bit down on the second one which actually helped get it all in his mouth.

After two weeks, Sugar was still so skinny, I asked the vet about it and he said that because she was so badly under-nourished due to the worms, it would take her awhile to recover. She was eating and drinking well, so I hoped she would start putting on weight soon. However, the vet considered her well enough to receive her first vaccination, so that was a good sign.

Sugar finally improved and put on weight. Her coat softened and she was much more active. She was no longer content to just sit in my lap anymore, she wanted to go down and explore.

Chloe stopped trashing her crate every night, was spayed and released.

Both kittens tamed up well and found their forever homes.

DQ Cat

One day, a resident noticed a pregnant cat eating out of the dumpster at a local fast food restaurant. The area was all retail locations, no homes nearby, so with approval from the restaurant manager, we set a trap. The resident and I took turns checking it and we were able to trap momma cat.

It was perfect timing trapping DQ when we did as she had her kittens the next night. I'm so glad we got her in time because I can't imagine trying to raise kittens in that location with all the heavy traffic.

DQ had four kittens, three orange tabbies like herself and one brown tabby. DQ had access to the entire downstairs bathroom, but it didn't look like she had moved from the crate all night. She looked exhausted.

When I walked into the room to do food, water and litter box duties, DQ usually laid on top of the kittens so I couldn't see them. I always had to get into the room quickly to do a head count before she covered them. She was a great mother, but she really freaked out when I was in the room. If I got too close to her and the kittens, she headed to higher ground, which is on top of the shower frame or a fan I have mounted near the ceiling by the door. While this would get me a good view of the kittens,

I hated to stress her out too much, especially since they were still so young.

Eventually, DQ and kittens were moved out to the condo crates and I covered the top portion of the crate with towels so DQ had a place to hide when I let the kittens out to play. After the kittens were weaned and put up for adoption, DQ was spayed and released into an established feral cat colony.

At Last

After trying for over a year, I finally trapped a pretty petite calico. All her siblings had already been trapped at about eight weeks of age, tamed and adopted and I just couldn't get the final one into a trap. That same night I wasn't only successful in getting her trapped, but her two young kittens as well. A great end to a long day.

Then, surprise! There was a third kitten. The resident had only seen two kittens with the calico mother, but a third kitten turned up and I was able to trap him. There are no other intact females on the property, and the third kitten was the same size as the others, so I wasn't sure where he had been hiding out. Momma, At Last, and all three kittens were now reunited.

Then we started Extreme Feral Kitten Taming Bootcamp! The third kitten, Dru, was a challenge to tame compared to his littermates. He had been on his own for four days before he was discovered and trapped. His littermates tamed up quickly and after they went up for adoption I could concentrate all of my energy on Dru. Then, I finally got the stubborn guy to purr for me. Whew. There was light at the end of the tunnel.

Taming feral kittens is a lot of work. It takes a lot of time and patience, neither of which is always in abundant supply. They hiss and spit and scratch and bite. However, when you finally have a feral kitten purring in your lap, it makes it all worthwhile. When I received a successful purr from the tough little guy, it melted my heart.

Taming improved after that point and Dru was finally ready to go up for adoption.

Cowyan and Tavin

A local humane society contacted me about two orange tabby cats that were surrendered as "indoor" cats. However, the cats were wild and already neutered and ear-tipped. The humane society was curious if the cats were from one of our colonies so I checked my records and they weren't any I had ever trapped. I offered to take them in, get them acclimated to the outdoor temperatures because it was winter, and release them into a colony. The cats came with no vet records, so I tested them for feline leukemia and vaccinated them.

It's always difficult relocating cats. One of the things I had to consider is that these two boys were kept indoors, so relocating them in winter wasn't ideal. They had been getting acclimated to the cooler temps in my garage, but I was still reluctant to release them outside with all the snow. After much searching, I was able to find an ideal option. They would be placed in an enclosed barn with a colony of cats I had already trapped and they would be provided food and water daily by the home owner.

Cowyan and Tavin were released into their new colony. They are sharing a huge barn with several other feral cats and if they want to venture outside, they have ten acres to roam. It will take a bit of time for them to adjust to the new living arrangements, but they were at least inside, warm, dry and had plenty of food and fresh water to enjoy.

Van

I had trapped over 20 feral cats at a hobby farm. The owners had recently purchased the farm without realizing it came complete with a colony of feral cats living in the barn. The first time I trapped there was a sick kitten and several pregnant females in one room in the barn. They weren't being cooperative going into the traps, so I spent my time crawling and lying on the floor, trying to net them as they navigated the tunnels of bales set up for their comfort. The floor was covered in straw, food, urine and feces. Even under these types of conditions, I enjoy getting the cats so they can be sterilized and stop the cycle of breeding. The last cat from this colony was finally trapped. I had left a trap with the resident and he had been trying to get the last hold out for weeks.

The feral looked like a Turkish Van cat, but very beat up. Turkish Van cats are beautiful white long-haired cats with a v-shape of color on the head and the same color tail. Van had the long-white fur and orange markings on his head and an orange tail, but he was not beautiful; he was dirty and scarred. All the other twenty plus cats in the colony had been trapped and sterilized, so Van must have been visiting cats in neighboring rural homes because he wasn't looking good. He was covered in scars and had bald spots with missing fur. He refused to look up for anything, so I was only able to get a picture of the top of his scared head.

Poor Van. In order to clean and treat his wounds, the veterinarian had to shave him while he was out for the neuter. It took his long coat awhile to grow back, but once his hormones leveled out, he wasn't scrapping with other cats anymore.

Feral Cat Trapping as a Spectator Sport

I love my solitude. I'm the ultimate wall flower, because I prefer to be invisible. Being the center of attention makes me very uncomfortable and interacting with people drains me.

Trapping feral cats has taken me out of my comfort zone on so many levels. Working with the cats, even when they are trying to do damage to me, is the easy part. Working with the people can be challenging: Educating some on why the cats should be allowed to live, and convincing others that spaying/neutering is the best course of action for the beloved feral cats they have been feeding for years. However, walking around with a trap and a net tends to draw attention so it's difficult for me to fly under the radar and just do what I need to do.

It was June and I had been called to a neighboring town to trap an orange tabby feral momma cat and her four kittens, all orange tabbies as well. The kittens were about eight weeks old and the entire family was living under a deck in an apartment complex for older residents. The deck where momma cat and her kittens were living was on the ground floor, about six inches off the ground, with an opening about three inches. I had to lie on my stomach in the grass, holding a flash light in order to see under the deck. There were no kittens under the deck. I set the traps anyway and as I walked back to my truck, I could hear a kitten meowing in the lower parking lot. When I looked over the railing, I saw momma cat running across the parking lot into a stand of pine trees next to a retaining wall. The kitten was crying for its mother as it tried to follow, but it retreated back into the safety of some bushes. Luckily, I was able to net the kitten and put her in a carrier in the truck.

Then I went after momma cat. I went to set traps where she was hiding, but the tree was a pine with branches all the way to the ground. As I stood trying to determine the best course of action, I learned that feral cat trapping had become a spectator sport in the complex. A resident called from a nearby balcony to tell me she saw the cat go under the tree. As I turned to thank her, I noticed that almost every deck had at least one person watching the activity below. The residents started asking questions and offering encouragement. I had to crawl under the pine tree in order to set the traps and the needles were scratching my arms and face. I was sweating and in combination with the dirt, the mixture was beginning to turn to mud on my clothing. I had a quick flashback to Air Force basic training and crawling through the sand pit with the canned machine gun fire going overhead. When I finally stood back up, I was filthy, hot and sweaty. Along with grass stains and dirt turning to mud, pine needles were stuck to the sweat on my body. What a time to have so many eyes on me.

I was able to finally trap momma cat and the other kittens.

The orange kittens, three females and one male, did well in their taming. Of course the male, Julius, tamed up the quickest which is always true for feral kittens. All four let me pick them up and hold them without any hissing. No one purred yet, so there was still a ways to go. They didn't approach me for attention, but when I walked into the room Julius was always at the door of the condo crate asking to be let out.

Tang, Crush and Julius all went up for adoption and momma cat was released into an established colony.

I decided to keep Fizz. Fizz had fallen down a sewer before she was trapped and suffered a head injury. The fire department actually saved her from the drain. Due to the head injury, Fizz's body trembled, she walked with high steps as if she was marching and she had difficulty focusing. Eating and jumping were a challenge. When eating, Fizz had to move her head back and forth, trying to focus on each kernel of food she attempted to eat. She often over or under shot when jumping on the couch and hit her head often. I once asked the vet if there was any type of helmet I could put on her. I didn't feel comfortable putting Fizz up for adoption because many people probably wouldn't want a kitten with head issues and I could make sure she received any medical care she needed as part of my furkid family. My cat Maze loved having a kitten to care for. Maze must have been a mother herself before she was rescued because she loved kittens and made sure they were always clean.

Unfortunately, I lost my Orange Fizz after only two years. She was my dog Qwincy's best friend. Fizz developed seizures which caused her to be aggressive to Qwincy, her cat housemates and me. The veterinarian did a lot of research before we made the final decision to let Fizz go. She now has a perfectly functioning brain which allows her to enjoy her life to the fullest.

Berta

I was trapping at a rural location and found two newborn kittens in a shed. I set traps for momma cat, but with no luck. I decided to leave the traps set over night and took the kittens home. Realizing that I didn't have any kitten formula at home, I detoured to the local pet store. Unfortunately, I arrived five minutes after they closed. Luckily, they still allowed me to buy kitten formula after I showed them the kittens through the window.

I bottle fed the kittens every two hours during the night. They had great appetites.

The resident called later the next day saying momma cat was finally in the trap. Momma and kittens were now reunited in my downstairs bathroom. I was happy they were back together and I was looking forward to a full night of sleep with no more feedings every two hours.

Momma cat, Berta, was a brown tabby and both kittens; Cayenne and Pepper, were solid black. After a week, Berta's kittens eyes opened. I handled the kittens several times a day, but they were taking cues from their momma and they often hissed at me. Hisses are so adorable at that age.

Berta was released back into her home territory after the kittens were weaned because he didn't like being in captivity. She hissed and lunged at me every time I got near the crate. It was quite the challenge cleaning the cat condo crate she was in with the kittens, and getting the kittens out daily to socialize. When I released her though, she didn't want to come out of the carrier, so I just left the door open for her to take her time.

Cayenne was a busy kitten. She would sit in laps for short periods of time, but if there was activity in the room, she had to be involved in the fun. Cayenne was very independent and confident. She liked wand toys and was super quick climbing up and down the cat tower. Cayenne liked to investigate and was very curious and was vocal when she played. At times it sounded like she was being hurt by the kitten she was playing with, but when checked, she was fine. She was just vocal while wrestling.

Pepper was more reserved than her littermate. She enjoyed sitting in laps and would stay for extended periods of time and loved having her ears massaged. If you rubbed her neck, she would sometimes move her foot like a dog does when you rub its belly. Pepper had access to many cat toys, but she seemed to prefer paper strips or paper balls. Pepper would sit back and watch activity for awhile, before joining in the fun. She took a little bit of time to warm up to new people, but once she did, she was a sweetheart.

Torpedo

Torpedo was a gray male cat who didn't like being in captivity. He would trash his crate every night with food, water, litter and newspaper everywhere.

One day after Torpedo trashed his crate the night before and I moved him to a clean one, he sprayed me for my trouble. Male cats spray urine to mark territory and in times of duress they will also spray. Unneutered male cat urine has a very strong, rancid smell. I hadn't been sprayed for some time, so I forgot how lovely the odor is when wearing it.

Torpedo finally went to the veterinarian and was tested for feline leukemia, vaccinated, de-parasited, neutered and ear-tipped. I was looking forward to releasing him as soon as possible to avoid any further incidents when moving him to clean crates, but with the turn of the weather, I had to hold off for a few days. The Torpedo Adventures continued!

Raccoons, Opossums and Skunks ...

Oh My!

One day, I started the morning on skunk duty. I had left a trap for a resident to try to get the last remaining feral cat on her property and I told her if she trapped overnight, she would likely get a raccoon, opossum or skunk. I received a call early the next morning from the resident saying she had a skunk in the trap and she was having trouble opening the trap to release it.

The resident had a piece of cardboard up against the trap so the skunk wouldn't spray her, but at that angle, she couldn't open the trap. On my way to work, I stopped by the location, walked very quietly up to the trap (no cardboard on my side), opened the trap and put in a dowel to hold it open. The skunk showed no inclination to come out of the trap so I left the trap blocked open and went to work. Eventually, the skunk left the trap on its own.

I was just so very happy not to be sprayed. I didn't want to add 'sprayed by skunk' to my list of reasons for working from home, the flea incident was enough.

Taz

The only way I can describe this black kitten was a category four tornado in a little fur suit. She got away from me three times trying to get her from the trap into the crate. She gave me a quite a workout, and left my heart pounding for several minutes after I got her into the crate. After her, the adult cat I trapped at the same time was very anti-climatic; she walked from the trap into the crate with no issues.

Taz it was. She was still very freaked out the following morning. I just entered the downstairs bathroom and she started whirling around in her crate. I was going to do a gender check and take pictures that morning, but I decided to wait until after work and hopefully she would calm down by then.

I was very relieved when Taz was finally vetted and spayed, and I could release her.

Feeding Ferals

Even with the snowshoes on, I sometimes sink into snow up to my knees getting out to the feral cat colonies to feed and I have to dig out the food and water bowls after a new snowfall. If I was lucky, a squirrel would already have started digging for the food bowl, so I knew where to go to get it out. There aren't usually many cat tracks right after a snowfall; everyone stays inside recovering from the snow storm.

I feed extra rations to feral cats in anticipation of some blizzards because potentially I may not be able to make it to the colonies until the roads are cleared. With the amount of snow and the nasty blowing wind, they usually don't venture out to eat anyway.

Many animals besides the feral cats will eat at the feeding stations: Deer, turkeys, raccoons, skunks, opossums, rabbits, squirrels, mice and birds. I love wild animals, but I can't afford to feed them too! At least when it's cold, the raccoons and opossums semi-hibernate, so I only see their tracks when it gets above freezing.

Yes, it is possible to spoil feral cats. I usually feed them moist food as a treat on Sundays during the year. In the fall, in preparation for the cold of winter, I feed moist food more often. The feral cats get very used to the treat of moist food and on days that only dry food is provided, they will sit and look at me with disdain, waiting for the good stuff. A few of them will even follow me back to the truck, hoping I will relent, and sometimes I do. It is hard to resist those little faces.

Momma Cat
'Bout Time

After two years of trying, I finally trapped a very prolific breeder, called Momma Cat by her human caretaker. I had tamed several litters of her kittens and I'm happy that both Momma Cat and I could rest now with her breeding days at an end.

I had tried every conceivable type of bait to get this cat in the trap. I tried the old standbys, moist cat food, mackerel and fried chicken. Then I moved to yogurt, milk, cream, pumpkin, catnip and hamburgers. I don't recall what bait finally got her into the trap, but it was a long time coming.

I tamed up 'Bout Time's last litter of kittens, Pounce, Peek and Puff. They were approximately eight weeks old when they were trapped and they were all brown tabbies like her, so when they got going it was just a blur of brown.

Pounce was a short-haired cat with polydactyl toes on the front paws. Polydactyl paws have extra toes so the cat's feet are huge. Some cats have all four paws as polydactyl and some only two. She liked to climb into laps and help on the computer when she had a chance. She was very energetic and playful. She loved to climb high on the cat tower and enjoyed toys and objects that make noise.

Peek was also short-haired cat with polydactyl toes on the front paws. Initially, Peek was very timid, but she became very outgoing and friendly. Peek preferred toys she could carry in her mouth.

Puff was a medium-hair and the only kitten in the litter without polydactyl toes. She was the most adventurous of the litter, but the other two kittens were quick to follow her lead. Puff liked to explore, climb and enjoyed wand toys. Puff didn't like to be confined to the kitten play area of my basement. Whenever I stepped over the baby gate to work on crafts or use the restroom, she would soon be underfoot, wanting to see what I was doing. Plus I had to share the computer chair with her. Actually it was more like she shared it with me.

Mr. Annabelle

Mr. Annabelle was found as a young kitten in a suburban backyard adjacent to a wooded lot. Two young girls who lived in the house on the property started playing with the orange tabby kitten and named it Annabelle.

Unfortunately, the family wasn't able to keep the kitten due to allergies in the family. They were directed to contact me and I went to pick up the kitten. I did a gender check and discovered Annabelle was a male and not wanting to disappoint the girls in their selection of a name, I added the prefix, Mr.

The young girls did a great job taming Mr. Annabelle. He was very sweet, playful and easy to handle. He was too busy to be a lap cat at that point, but he was fine being held and carried for short periods of time.

Mr. Annabelle was popular with the staff at the veterinary clinic and again later at the mobile spay/ neuter unit. He was very personable, outgoing and lovable. He played well with Qwincy and other kittens.

Mr. Annabelle was adopted to a great home and became a much loved indoor cat. He was lucky to have had two little girls to get him started on the good life or he may have ended up being another feral cat statistic. The current statistic is that there are 50 million feral cats in the U.S. This is not just a U.S. issue though. The largest number of feral cats in one location is reported to be in Rome, Italy with an estimate of 350,000. Luckily, TNR is an international program and is practiced worldwide to help reduce the number of feral cats.

OMGoodness – What a Cluster!

A resident had kindly taken in two feral female cats, as well as a stray male during the winter months. The male got to work and surprise, two months later, there were eight kittens under the bed. The resident contacted the local rescue agency, but there weren't willing to keep the two feral momma cats until the kittens were old enough to be weaned, so they called me.

I went to the resident's home after work on the day I received the call. The ten-day-old kittens were snug in a box. Unfortunately, the feral mothers weren't. The feral cats had the run of the house. Let us just say there was sweat, nets, scratches, bites and fresh cat urine involved.

I had brought gloves and nets and we put them to good use. We finally blocked the two momma cats into the bedroom – and there wasn't much room to move in there. There were piles of clothes lining the entire room, with a small path to the bed. It took about 10 minutes to get momma cat number one netted and removed from under the bed. Momma cat number two had crawled under a dresser. It still never ceases to amaze me how cats can cram their bodies into such small spaces.

It was too cramped under the dresser to get the net over the cat completely, so it took about 20 minutes to get her out. I'm used to having cats urinate on me, but I think she saved up two days worth to pee down my leg and onto the floor when I finally got her out. Of course I had come directly from work, so I was wearing dress pants. I was sweating by the time we were done, had several scratches and one bite and I was totally exhausted. I usually don't drink during the week, because alcohol disrupts my sleep and I need to be alert for work, but I treated myself to a large glass of wine that night! The pants went directly into the trash.

There had been communal nursing going on with the two momma cats, so the resident wasn't sure which kittens went with which mother. They were born only a day apart, so they were all the same size. The condo crates I use aren't big enough for two growing families, so I split them down the middle and everyone did well with the momma cat they were assigned.

I had been able to handle the kittens from both litters. Momma cat number one would lie still and growl at me, but she let me take them. Momma cat number two hissed, growled and swatted at me. Then she would jump up to one of the higher levels of the condo crate and scowl at me until I was done.

As the kittens got older and came out of the crates to play. I made sure to put the same kittens in with the same mom since they grew comfortable with the arrangement. One day after I had put the kittens back into the crates, one of the kittens looked very confused and not sure what to do or where to go. I quickly realized I had put him in the wrong crate, so I switched the two misplaced kittens and the kitten was good to go with his familiar surroundings.

71

One morning momma cat number two decided not to jump to the upper level of the cat condo crate when I opened it to let the kittens out. After the hiss, growl and swat, she bit me. Luckily I was wearing gloves so there was no damage done. Nothing like a cat bite to wake you up in the morning.

Two of the kittens were undersized and I bottle fed them to supplement what they were getting from the momma cats. The gray kitten took the bottle like a champ but I had to use an eye-dropper with the white kitten as he didn't like the bottle. Of course, he was the smallest of the small.

Unfortunately, both undersized kittens passed away. One of the kittens passed away in my hands. It is always so devastating to lose kittens. I know I should think of the 300+ cats I helped, but at the time I could only think of the little ones I lost.

All the remaining kittens found good homes and the two momma cats were released into the same feral cat colony.

College Cats

I had been contacted about a small colony of cats at a local college. The students were leaving food for the cats and had even put straw under some equipment trailers for the cats to sleep on. One of the parents contacted me to help the cats. The college wanted the cats trapped and removed.

Usually when trapping, we check the traps every hour or two. However, it was winter, bitterly cold and the college was a good drive from my home, so I had to stay to ensure the cats didn't get too cold in the trap. The traps were metal, but I had a towel in the trap and they were well covered with blankets on top. It was so cold I had to keep the truck running so I would stay comfortable as well. Luckily, I could get email, facebook and games on my cellular phone, so I was able to remain entertained while I waited. Sitting and watching traps is like waiting for water to boil in a kettle, nothing seems to happen when you stare.

When the cats weren't eating by the dumpsters, they seemed to be living in the dry swamp area below the college. The snow was so deep I sank up to my hips, so I had to wear snow shoes in order to trap in that location. It was amazing how the cats could navigate in the dead long grass and many feet of snow. It was hard keeping the food tantalizing in the cold. We usually use moist cat food, tuna or mackerel, all of which freeze quickly in the deep freeze of a frigid winter. I kept the food warm by putting in on the dash of my truck and running the heater on high. I had to put new food in the traps about every hour to keep it from freezing.

I eventually trapped all seven cats, along with a skunk. I generally don't trap at night since that's when the raccoons, opossums and skunks are out, but in winter in the northern states, there isn't much daylight to work with so trapping in the dark is a necessity. Luckily, the skunk wasn't too worked up in the trap and walked out quietly after I had blocked the trap open. After being vetted and sterilized, all the cats were relocated to other established colonies. One cat, Tiara, a beautiful Calico, had kittens shortly after she was trapped.

Tiara

I enjoyed the sounds of feral momma cat, Tiara, making comforting noises to her kittens. It's different than purring, more of a hum and twitter combination and s much better than the hissing and growling while swatting at me she did earlier when I was taking the kittens out for playtime.

Tiara was trapped at a local college and soon after I got her settled in the downstairs bathroom, she had kittens.

Kittens Tia, Tonka and Trey grew quickly. They had access to dry kitten food at all times, and were fed moist food twice a day. One morning, Tia decided that she didn't want to wait until playtime was over to have her moist food, so she started to help herself. She was able to get one canine tooth through the top of the foil lid of the moist cat food.

Tonka would meow for attention. I would pick him up and pet him for awhile and then put him back down. Soon, he would jump from the cat tower right onto my laptop - he always wanted more attention than I gave him. He definitely had my attention when landing on my lap.

When Trey wanted attention, he liked to climb up my pant leg when I was sitting at the computer, so he could sit in my lap. I never minded, except for the times I was wearing shorts and he still climbed up my leg.

Tia, Tonka and Trey were adopted together into one home. They were able to stay together and grow up in a loving home. Who could ask for more? Their mother, Tiara, was spayed and vaccinated and released into an established colony since she couldn't be returned to the college.

Every time kittens born to a feral mother get good homes, I think about what their life would have been like if momma cat hadn't been trapped. Would the kittens have survived? How healthy would they be scrounging for food? Would they spend most of their day being scared? How long and comfortable would their life be? It is so rewarding to know that those three kittens' had a good outcome. And for feral momma cat, she won't have any more kittens, the feral cat colony she will be released to has food, water and shelter and she has a human caretaker looking out for her welfare.

No live Trapping…
Kitten 1, Clarissa 0!

I was working with a resident who didn't believe in using live traps to trap feral cats. She had a bad experience with a feral cat that freaked out in the trap and injured itself. I found out later that the resident hadn't covered the trap with a towel, which helps calm them down. As it turns out, the resident was okay with using nets and a catch pole, which is more time consuming and I feel, more traumatic to the animal because they are being restrained bodily, rather than being allowed to move freely in a trap.

In order to respect the resident's wishes, I was using catch poles and nets trying to get the feral kittens that lived under her trailer home. The kittens were about eight weeks old and very agile and fast. It was hot out, so I took off my gloves and one of the kittens I grabbed with the pole bit down very hard on my thumb. For a kitten bite, it sure hurt and took about 30 minutes to stop bleeding. My thumb throbbed and grew larger than it should have been. Of course, the kitten got away. I've been bitten many times, but never by a cat/kitten that also got away. Luckily, I'm vaccinated against rabies.

After the thumb incident, the resident agreed to live trapping. She felt awful for my injury. I finally was able to trap two feral kittens, but not the one that bit me. And, it wasn't an easier experience with the traps, because the resident was so nervous about using them, she checked the traps often making the cats nervous and they stayed away.

The two brown tabby feral kittens we trapped were named Wisha (short for wish upon a star) and Wurcher. They were approximately eight weeks old when trapped and tamed up nicely for adoption.

We never did trap the kitten that bit me.

Raisin

I received a call from a resident in a neighboring town about a cat he found in the wheel well of his truck after he returned from work. She was very pregnant and dripping, so he thought she was about to give birth. The city police gave him our information and I went to pick her up after work. She was solid black and I named her Raisin.

Raisin gave birth about a week later. She had no microchip and flyers sent to local veterinarians and postings to online lost and found sites generated no owner.

I didn't think petite Raisin would have room for more than three kittens in her tiny body, but the morning I found that she had given birth, she had six good-sized kittens to proudly show me. I have no idea how she fit them all in there. Raisin was a very friendly momma cat, which was nice because that doesn't happen often and it's fun to have an easy interaction with momma and kittens.

Raisin's kittens were the most unusual color I have ever seen on a cat. I looked through my cat book and the closest coloration I could find was on a Blue Point Mitted. The Blue Point is a beautiful blue/gray color with white "mitted" paws. However, as they got older, the gray areas turned black, so I thought Raisin's kittens must be part Ragdoll. Also, every time I picked them up they just went limp, especially the biggest one, Klondike. I would put him on his back on my arm and he would just lay there and look up at me for the longest time. Ragdolls get their names from the fact that when picked up, they go limp and relaxed, like a ragdoll. Ragdolls are large cats with beautiful markings and a luxurious coat of medium-length fur. Ragdolls have very sweet temperaments and are very affectionate.

The play area never seemed big enough for Klondike. He was always trying to go around or over the baby gate to see what was beyond that "huge fence." Since he was so big and such an adventurer, Klondike seemed like the perfect name for him. Klondike took a shine to Qwincy, and I had a feeling Qwincy and Klondike would be too good at making trouble together given the chance.

I have dozens of kittens go through my house every year and although I get attached, I'm usually glad when they hit eight weeks and can go up for adoption. They are a lot of work, but once in a while though, a kitten seems to pick me and I find it difficult to say no. That is what was happening with Little Miss Duchess. Believe me, all the kittens received lots of attention, but it just seemed like Little Miss Duchess would sneak into my lap more often than the others. Plus, the other kittens didn't give me "the look" like she did. "The look" was just an innocent kitten gazing into my eyes that seemed to speak volumes, as if trying to make a connection. I knew I could easily get drawn into that look, so I broke eye contact when possible. Despite her best efforts to win my heart and a place in my home, I knew I wouldn't be able to keep her.

The rest of the kittens also each had their own personalities: Elise liked to be up high, so she was a climber. However, sometimes she would get stuck and had to be helped back down. No Blanc, the only kitten without white markings, liked to climb and chase shadows on the wall. Rosca loved attention and loved to play, so she was always reluctant to go back into the crate after play time was over. Greta was the most independent of the kittens. She would sit in laps for short periods of time, but there was too much to do and see to sit still for long.

Raisin and her kittens all received forever homes, except one was destined to come back into my life.

Klondike

Yes, Raisin's kitten Klondike has a separate story and you can probably guess he's the one that came back into my life.

Klondike's adopted family returned him to the rescue agency due to aggressive behaviors. I'm not sure how a family can adopt a ten-week-old, friendly, outgoing kitten and return him five months later because he is a terrified, aggressive cat. The rescue agency asked if I could evaluate Klondike, so he came back to my home.

The adoptive family reported that Klondike was aggressive with cat and people food and he wouldn't stay off the counters and table. They also said he beat up their cat and urinated behind the couch. Finally they reported that if Klondike was given more than a half a cup of food, he would have diarrhea.

The family said they tried everything, so I assumed they also took him to the veterinarian. But, when I received the vet records I found that he had only been to the veterinary once since he was adopted and that was to be declawed. I took Klondike to the veterinarian right away and even they were surprised he was returned as aggressive. I knew I had to see what was going on with Klondike if he was going to have any chance of being adopted again, so I tried to replicate each of the family's complaints.

My first priority was to understand the food aggression claim. When an animal is food aggressive, they growl and hiss and can potentially attack any other animal, and sometimes humans, if they come near their food. They are protective of their food and treats and can cause injury if they feel their food source is threatened. It is a very dangerous situation, especially if there are children in the house. I started by offering Klondike a small piece of cheese and when he started to take it gently I took it away from him. Then, I offered it again, took it away again and on the third offering, he still took it gently and I let him eat it. When Klondike ate his regular meal and Qwincy and the other cats were near him, he didn't do anything to indicate he even noticed them. The same thing happened when he had kittens crawling up and over his crate while he was eating: he didn't seem to notice them. Not once did Klondike show any kind of aggressive behavior.

Second, I took Klondike to the veterinarian to understand why he might have diarrhea after eating. The vet found that there was an elevated bacteria level in his intestines which increases with stress thus producing diarrhea. With medication and prescription cat food, Klondike's GI tract went back to normal. If the family had taken him to the vet, they would have found the problem with his GI tract and he would have been more comfortable.

Next, I outfitted Klondike with a harness and leash (just in case) to test interacting with my furkids. Klondike initiated play with Fizz and

Qwincy and the other cats ignored him, except for Cricket. Cricket did approach him while hissing and growling but Klondike's reaction was to immediately look away and lay down. He actually seemed rather comfortable with everyone right away. He even would lay down with his stomach exposed when all the cats were in the same room. I was amazed that he would lay on his side and back, exposing his tummy to my cats so soon. The cat's stomach is very tender and vulnerable. When a cat exposes its stomach to another animal or a human, it shows complete trust and that they feel safe and comfortable.

Counter Surfing was next. I once had a cat that was into everything food related, so he taught me not to leave any food out and to put dirty dishes in the dishwasher immediately. So my counters and table aren't very exciting but we started on a leash around the house just in case. Klondike didn't try to jump up on the counters or the table, but he did pull over a glass of water on the end table when he was sitting on my lap on the couch. Luckily I caught it before anything spilled and I just chalked it up to kitten curiosity and my having the glass too close to the edge.

Finally, I monitored him to see if he was peeing behind the couch. Klondike used the litter box consistently and has never gone to the bathroom outside the box.

Klondike quickly graduated to full run of the house.

After all that, I figured that Kondike was nervous in that house for some reason. Maybe the other cat was aggressive toward Klondike so he felt he had to protect his food, fight back, and wasn't comfortable using the litter box. My cats are used to other cats, so he didn't feel threatened, even by crabby Cricket, and he seemed very comfortable in my home.

I reported back to the rescue agency that neither I, nor the veterinarian could find any aggression issues with Klondike. When the agency asked if I would put him up for adoption again, I hesitated. The poor guy has been through so much and I didn't think it would be right to make him adjust to another home and family. Also, I had wanted to keep him all those months ago when he was a kitten and now that he was back in my life, I knew it was meant to be. I considered Klondike to be home so he became a permanent part of my fur family.

Klondike makes me laugh every day. He still goes limp when I pick him up, just like when he was a kitten. He follows me around like a little dog and is so close underfoot that if I stop quickly or step backward; I tend to step on him. He has such a fascination with the bathtub, that when I start the shower in the morning I often have to lift him out of the tub first. He is also a great snuggler and very affectionate. I'm glad he is back, even though he had to suffer to get here.

Spurs
(aka) Slider

I was asked to trap a feral momma cat and her five kittens that were living in a resident's garage. I was able to get momma cat and the five kittens rather quickly, but when I was getting ready to leave, I noticed another white kitten. The resident told me there was only one white kitten, so I checked the traps in the back of the truck to make sure the white kitten hadn't escaped. He was still there, so it looked like there were actually two white kittens. I had used all six traps I had in my truck, but I wasn't leaving without the last kitten. I gave the resident a net, I used a grabber and after maneuvering in the cluttered garage for some time, we were finally able to corner and net the kitten.

The two white kittens looked like they may be Siamese mixes and had such tiny, blue eyes, I was worried that they had Micropthalmia, a condition were kittens have very small or uneven eye size. One of the white kittens also had severely crossed eyes. Pure bred Siamese cats can have crossed eyes, but the momma cat to this litter of kittens was an orange tabby. I did some reading on the internet about small eyes and it sounded like it was a problem with going blind later in life. However, the vet checked the eyes and ruled out Micropthalmia.

I was going to keep the cross-eyed Siamese, Slider, but since Klondike came back, I didn't think

I should add two new cats, so my sister adopted Slider and he is now known as Spurs. She needed a companion for her cat and thought Spurs would fit the bill. Spurs has limited peripheral vision so he startles easily and has difficulty focusing, but other than that he does well. He has no idea he has any issues, he is just as energetic and adventurous as any other kitten. He is quite the snuggler and gives kisses on the chin. Even with his eye condition, he FETCHES! The ball they use has a bell in it and Spurs brings it directly back to the thrower!

Spurs is now a beautiful flame-point color with a wonderful forever home. Flame-point cats have a white or cream body with a reddish coloration in their face, legs and tail. It is a beautiful coloration especially with the striking blue eyes.

The Cat Who Sits by Traps

One night, I was trapping at an established colony and I had re-trapped an already eartipped cat, but sitting next to the closed trap was a cat without an ear tip. I let the ear-tipped cat out, reset the trap and drove off a bit to see if the non ear-tipped cat would come back and enter the trap. After about 15 minutes I looked through the binoculars to check the trap and the non-ear-tipped cat was sitting next to the open trap, looking back at me. I think he may have even stuck its tongue out at me and said "pflt"!

Nasty Momma and her Adorable Kittens

I agreed to take in a very protective momma cat and her six kittens from a rescue agency in another part of the state. The momma cat wasn't feral, but she would attack whenever anyone got near the kittens. The rescue agency wanted someone who was used to aggressive mother cats and could work with the kittens so they were tame enough for adoption.

Momma cat let me pet her the first night. Later when I was adding food to the condo crate, she clocked me good in the eye. Luckily I blinked in time and she only got the eyelid. She opened up the eyelid pretty good, and I should probably have gone to the emergency room to get it stitched, but it was late, I was tired and the closest ER was a bit of a drive away. Instead, I covered it with a wet wash cloth and lay on the bed flat on my back until it stopped bleeding. It had been awhile since I had a momma cat that feisty, so it was back to dressing like a hockey goalie when I was near her. For the first few days my eye looked like I had been in a fist fight.

Momma cat wouldn't only swipe with claws when I got close, she would scream too. Usually I like to take the kittens out to play two or three times a day, but with this momma it was such a battle to get the kittens away from her, they were only getting out once a day to play. They were worth the battle though, cute and cuddly.

Momma cat was beautiful and when away from the kittens she was sweet. She was just very protective of her babies. It went better after I started mollifying her with moist food while I interacted with the kittens. She would still hiss and growl at me, but she didn't make the effort to lunge at me with extended claws while she was eating her beloved moist food.

I didn't name the kittens because they were going back to the agency once they were ready for adoption, but one had already been named Zippy, since she had stitches on her head after a scalp injury.

I gladly returned momma cat and her kittens to the rescue agency once the kittens were old enough for adoption.

Cold

I always worry about the feral cats when it gets bitterly cold outside. I feel better when they are in colonies, because when it's feeding time, they all come out of the same shelter, so I know they have been snuggled up and keeping each other warm.

The only thing that actually gets me out of the house on bone-chilling days is feeding the ferals. On days with bitter wind chills and eight plus inches of snow on the ground with more falling, it's very tempting to just stay inside. Then I think of the feral cats sitting and waiting patiently by their food dishes to fill their empty bellies and shake off the cold. That visual makes me get off my duff so I can fill their tummies with good food and fresh water. A hungry cat is always a great motivator!

Many people believe that outside cats will only live two to three years, but with improved health, proper food, water and shelter, they can live long and productive lives. Their health is improved by vaccinations and sterilizations. Females no longer have multiple litters of kittens each year that they must feed and protect, and males no longer have to fight over food, territory and females. Also, if one of the feral cats becomes sick, it is re-trapped and taken to the vet for care.

Saving Jasper

Jasper was a beautiful Siamese mix cat, but he wasn't so good looking the first time I saw him. When I first saw Jasper he was emaciated and severely wounded.

Jasper was abandoned outside after his family was evicted from their trailer court. By the time Jasper showed up at a feral cat feeding station in front of a cat caretaker home, he was dehydrated, emaciated and severely wounded in the back. The cat caretaker did some research and found out about the eviction, but she wasn't able to get a date on when it happened so we weren't sure how long Jasper was on his own.

Jasper spent a few days at the veterinarians being re-hydrated and treated for his infected wounds. Whatever got him, got him running away because all the wounds were on his back and sides. I think it may have been another cat or a raccoon. The raccoons in the trailer court where Jasper was found are huge. Jasper returned from the vet on antibiotics and high-calorie cat food to get some weight on him.

Once he was in better health, Jasper was vaccinated and neutered. Even though he was covered with fleas, he has no internal parasites. Luckily, Jasper was able to find a forever home.

BOHF
Big Orange Hissy Fit

I was trapping at a rural location and had trapped a cat by a dumpster in an alley. It was a big orange cat, hissing and spitting when he saw me. It was hard carrying him in the trap to my truck because he was raging around inside.

At home I got him from the trap and into the crate and took pictures. Unfortunately, I had taken off my gloves to use the camera and he came at me hissing and spitting again and got a claw in my finger. I will never learn - always wear gloves within a foot of the cage - they do have reach. He was holding his left ear at an angle due to ear mites and his left eye was cloudy with an ulcer.

Big Orange Hissy Fit (BOHF) was vetted, vaccinated, neutered and released back to the location where he was trapped.

Now Fast Forward. BOHF befriended a nearby resident's cat and unfortunately, the cat passed away soon after their friendship had started. It isn't known what type of communication these two cats shared as they laid together in the sun, but BOHF later invited himself into the resident's home and decided to stay. Now BOHF is known as Beaucephus and is a loving indoor cat. Okay, he still won't come near me, but he made his way into the hearts and home of his new family.

Conversation with a Crabby Guy

I had fed the same feral cat colony for five years and had never met this man before, but he claimed he had lived in the neighborhood for 30 plus years. I was just getting into my truck after feeding the colony and the man approached me and started talking.

Crabby Guy (CG): "Why don't you just take those cats away?"

Me: "Why? Many of them have been here for five years. They are all spayed and neutered."

CG: "There are too many of them."

Me: "There are actually fewer than when I started trapping. Also no kittens have been born at this location for three years now."

CG: "They kill the wildlife."

Me: "What wildlife have they killed?"

CG: "When I first moved here there were pheasants everywhere. Now, there are no pheasants."

Me: "When did you move here?"

CG: "1974."

CG: "They eat the pheasant eggs you know!"

Me: "I'm not sure a cat would know what to do with an egg. There are raccoons, opossums and skunks that live here too and I know that raccoons eat eggs."

CG: "They eat the pheasant chicks…"

Me: "That's possible, but I know that raccoons eat chicks."

CG: "…and they spread diseases!"

Me: "The cats here are all vaccinated, so they have no diseases to spread."

Crabby Guy turns around and stomps off.

Bella and Daisy

I was trapping in a new location in Chaska and an elderly resident had about five cats she was feeding. I trapped one adult, Bella, and one kitten, Daisy, who was about eight weeks old. Daisy had the prettiest yellow eyes and her fur was white, so she reminded me of a little Daisy flower.

Still M.I.A were an eight-week-old orange tabby kitten, an adult male, and an adult female that was nursing some young kittens somewhere in the yard. The resident had a shed, a garage and lots of junk in the yard, so the momma cat could have been hiding those kittens anywhere. I searched, hoping to at least hear kittens mewing, but I had no luck finding their location.

I was finally able to trap the second kitten, Currant, the daddy cat, Roman, and the three kittens the one mother had hidden, but the momma cat was refusing to get into the trap. I had actually trapped her several weeks earlier, but I could tell she was nursing kittens, so I had to let her go or the kittens would have starved. Now that the kittens were old enough to be on their own, the mother cat wouldn't get back into the trap. She was such a little thing too. I didn't want to see her keep turning out litters of kittens. The resident fed them well, but it is tough on that little body to keep having kittens.

After weeks of persistence, the last momma cat was trapped again and her breeding days ended with her spay. She was released back into the resident's yard to enjoy her new life.

Sydney

Sydney was a grey and white kitten trapped at a residence near my home. She didn't look good at all. She was lethargic, had green goo coming from her eyes and had wounds on her head and neck. With Sydney's wounds, it looked like she had been in some animal's mouth at one time. There were several dogs in the neighborhood that were allowed to run loose, plus a coyote had been sighted in that area too, so we weren't sure what had happened.

When Sydney went to the vet, we learned that her wounds weren't from teeth. She had a cuterebra, a parasitic slug, under her skin and the wounds were the entrance and exits from the slug. To this day, that was one of the grossest things I have encountered with ferals. Sydney's immune system was compromised from the parasite, so she was on meds for ten days. She was so lethargic it made applying medication to her eyes and shoving medication down her throat twice a day much easier. This also helped quite a bit in the taming process.

She luckily recovered quickly and went up for adoption. I have come across many cuterebras since then and they still make my skin crawl.

Phantom
The Cat not Trapped

The smart ones are tough! With certain cats it can take days or weeks to catch them, but I can be very persistent and I don't give up easily. There was one male cat, Phantom, who lived in the woods across the street that I tried to trap for two years.

I don't even remember when Phantom first showed up. The large, long-haired black cat would emerge from a culvert under the road every evening and though I had never actually seen him in the woods, he always appeared out of the culvert, so the woods had to be his starting point. Unless the culvert branched off somewhere under the road, but I wasn't going to crawl through to find out. He just sat by my bushes, waiting for me to get home from work to feed him.

Phantom always showed up once a day around five o'clock in the evening to eat. If I got home late from work, he would give me a look as if asking; "Where have you been?" He always retreated back to the culvert when I filled the food and water bowls, then he would come back out when I entered the house. He would cower from people and vehicles, running back to the culvert whenever he felt threatened. He was a beautiful cat. Well, I think it was a male. His long hair made a gender check impossible, but with his size and the fact that after two years there hadn't been any kittens accompanying him, he had to be a male.

I provided Phantom with food and water by the bush line in my front yard and when I started, I left an open trap there for days so he would get used to it. Then I gradually started to move the food into the trap toward the back. He flat out refused to go into the trap. He would plant his feet outside the trap and lean in as far as he could to get the food inside. I thought after a few days he would be hungry enough to go farther in, most cats do, but when he saw the food was too far to reach from his position outside, he would leave. He always came back though and after awhile I worried about his condition if he didn't eat so I gave in and fed him outside the trap again.

I used every food imaginable in the trap, but he wasn't even tempted by the smelly mackerel that most cats can't refuse. I put towels with other cats' scent into the trap, but he sniffed from the outside and that was enough. I even put a towel that a female cat in heat had laid on, but still no go. I tried everything I could think of, but after two years I decided Phantom had won and I admitted defeat.

Tough Day at the "Office"
Previously Published in the *Chaska Herald*

My toughest day with ferals was tax day, April 15, 2008. This story has nothing to do with taxes, but being tax day, it may have had some to do with the atmosphere that day.

It started by getting a tiny, gray female feral cat from the crate into the carrier to go to the veterinarian to be spayed. On the rare occasion a cat gets away from me, I'm usually able to net it within a short timeframe and get it into the carrier. This tiny, gray feral wasn't so easy. She got away in a quick gray flash. Of course, this happens in the garage, where everything was still stored from winter so there were lots of hiding places. After spending two hours literally moving every piece of anything in the garage, I still couldn't find her. Did she quietly move from one area to the next while I searched? I know she didn't get outside and I know she wasn't in the house since my dog and cats hadn't given an "intruder" alarm. So, I set three humane traps in the garage to catch her when she decided to come out.

Now, I have to explain that I worked from home that day only because I was afraid to open the garage door to get my car out, in case the feral cat got away. I did finally have to open the garage door that afternoon to go and pick up two feral cats at a local impound facility. I quickly opened the garage door, drove the car out and closed the door again, with no gray streaks going by.

It gets better. At the impound facility, the first feral cat gets away from me in the cat kennel room and goes up into the false ceiling. Can this possibly be happening to me twice in one day? The Animal Control Officer and I scratch our heads and try to track down the cat in the false ceiling. She finally came down, in the dog kennel room and we are able to net her and get her into a crate.

I then drive home, drive into the garage (no gray streaks) and even though I would like to relax, I still have to get the two feral cats from the carriers to the crates. They must be tired from the excitement at impound, since they cooperate and go into the crates without a fuss. Now I can relax and look back and hope I never have a day like today again.

And the little gray cat? She was trapped in a humane trap in the garage and returned to her crate. And the day she finally went to the vet? She put up a fight again resisting my efforts to move her from the crate to the carrier, but she didn't get away a second time. She is now tested, vaccinated, wormed, spayed and has been released back into her home territory under the care of a resident who provides her food, water and shelter. The little gray cat definitely wants to live! She was a tough little thing and I admired her for that trait.

Toots
Tootsie Roll

Pregnant feral cat Toots, was way out of my trapping area, but luckily the resident was willing to trap the cat and meet me halfway because it wasn't safe for the cat where she was currently residing.

The resident called her Toots, but I extended her name to Tootsie Roll because she had such a big middle and she was solid black. She was huge, so I expected that she would have her kittens soon. Toots wasn't a mean feral like some, but she definitely didn't like to be handled. She would always run and hide when approached. She wasn't very cooperative at the veterinarian during her checkup and she did get away from them in the exam room. However, because she wasn't very limber in her pregnant state, she was apprehended quickly.

Toots had six kittens, but one was born with its intestines outside of its body and didn't live. The remaining five did well and Toots was a great mother. She hissed and growled whenever I would go into the downstairs bathroom to feed, water and clean, but she did tolerate me doing a quick headcount to make sure everyone was doing well.

The night Toots had her kittens, it was very cold and damp, so Toots was lucky to have been trapped when she was, and her kittens were born indoors in warm and dry conditions.

104

All the kittens were black. Some had white markings on face and feet and a couple of them looked like they might be tortoise shells. Usually with feral moms, I don't handle the kittens until they are about two to three weeks old so I don't stress the mom. However, I did have to handle Toots' kittens after they were born. They were in my downstairs bathroom and I covered about 75 percent of the floor with towels for Toots to have her babies. Of course, she chose the uncovered 25 percent of the floor in front of the door and had her kittens on the cold linoleum. I did move the kittens to a towel and covered the rest of the floor with towels so if she moved them, the only choices were warm places.

Because I had been calling the momma cat Tootsie Roll, I gave all the kittens candy names. Jelly Bean was a black and white tuxedo and too young for a gender check, but the other four were tortoiseshells, so they were all female; Snickers, KitKat, Rolo and Hershey.

I moved the family from the downstairs bathroom to a multi-level condo crate in my craft room once the kittens became mobile. There wasn't as much room as in the bathroom, but this new arrangement allowed them to hear common household noises and get used to being part of a family. Once the kittens were steadier on their feet, they were brought out of the crate at least twice a day to play, socialize and learn to use the scratching post. Toots was great with me handling them. I was very impressed as most of the feral mommas hiss and growl when the kittens are approached. I was sitting in the bathroom with them one night and everything was so nice and calm, I forgot Toots was feral reached to pet her. She didn't like that at all but she still let me handle the kittens with no problems.

The kittens all went up for adoption and Toots was released to an established colony of cats after she was vetted and spayed.

Cricket
Therapy Cat

I trapped several feral kittens on a resident's property and the last one trapped, Cricket, was a black female and a little spitfire. The male kittens tamed up nicely and were ready for adoption soon, but Cricket needed more work.

From the moment I saw her in the crate, I felt as if Cricket was the missing member of my family. I've had many kittens go through my house and while many of them have touched my heart, I had no desire to keep any of them. However, I really felt a connection to Cricket and I couldn't bear to put her up for adoption. She had to get over a cold before she could integrate with the rest of the family. Once she was well she bunked with Qwincy in the kitchen until she could have the run of the house.

It took awhile for little kitten, Cricket, to finally be tamed. I finally could pet her and pick her up without her hissing, spitting and scratching. She even started meowing for attention.

I call Cricket my therapy cat because she became such a lap cat, cuddling up with me each evening when I sit on the couch to read or watch TV. She loves being on my lap and getting petted. She tries to help me on the computer too. She loves watching and batting at the cursor on the screen.

Besides Cricket, three of my cats like to be petted. Izzabelle and Journey move constantly while they are being petted, walking back and forth, turning this way and that, so it isn't very relaxing to pet them. Then there is Maze who just sits on my lap like a brick. Cricket on the other hand likes to curl up against my neck when I pet her and she snuggles in and purrs loudly. At bedtime, she curls up in front of my face and gently pats my face with her paw a few times before she falls asleep. The scene is extra special when you realize that her life started out as a feral kitten. If she wasn't napping pleasantly in my home, she would already have had several litters of kittens and she would be outside with them, trying to scrounge up enough to eat and drink before finding a safe and warm place to spend the night.

Winston

Well, I knew it was a boy the minute I started walking down the stairs to the basement the morning after I trapped him. I could smell him and without doing a gender check I knew it was a male cat. I have never been able to understand how people can tolerate an unneutered male cat in their home; the smell is strong and overpowering. Since unneutered male cats spray to mark territory, their urine has a very strong and rancid odor. Once the male cat is neutered and the hormones diminish, so does the smell. With older cats it can take several months for the odor to reduce to the standard cat urine smell.

I named the cat Winston and he hissed at me whenever I got close. I generally put the smelly boys in crates in the garage so I can breathe in the house.

When I transfer a cat from the trap to a crate, I have everything ready to go in the new accommodations; food, bed and litter box. I wait to add water until after the transfer, because it always seems to get spilled and I hate to leave a cat in a wet crate. The transfer of Winston from trap to crate went well. I couldn't get him to move at first, so it took awhile, but it went smoothly, meaning there was no escape attempt. I left the room and just a few minutes later I heard the metal food and water dishes rattling and it hit me, "Oh, I forgot to fill the water!" I went back into the room and Winston was sitting right in front of the water dish and gave me such a withering look;

"You FORGOT something!" and it made me laugh. He moved to the back of the crate when I filled the water, but he still gave me that disappointed look.

Nez
Many Benefits of Spaying

Cats are very good at masking illness.

Nez was a pretty black and white tuxedo cat. Her one distinct marking was the white blaze that ran down the front of her face, not centered, but off to the right side. It looked like the marking had slid off the middle and ended up under her right eye.

Nez was a little female, and one of the nastiest cats I had ever dealt with. Whenever I got within a foot of her crate, she was running at me hissing and spitting until she hit the door. Swapping out her litter box and providing food and water was a challenge every day. The water was easier. If the dish was clean I poured water into the dish from the outside. I hadn't found a good way to do this with food without making a mess, but I tried.

Despite all my other efforts, he door absolutely had to be opened for the litter box swap. Complete with gloves and a long sleeve shirt, I crouched in front of the crate and quickly opened the door, took out the litter box and closed the door just as Nez would come at me, slamming her body against the crate door. I then had to wait until she retreated to the back of the crate and repeat the same process while putting the clean litter box back in.

On the day she was spayed, the veterinarian called to tell me that the surgery went well and that Nez had pyometra. Pyometra is an infection in the uterus and can be fatal if not treated. The spay removes the diseased organs and an injection helps clean up the infection. Lucky for Nez, the spay surgery saved her life and she is now back with her colony.

The Three Tortoiseshells

It had been an amazing year for tortoiseshell kittens. I couldn't remember the last time I had a tortoiseshell kitten, but that year I had five so far. Tortoiseshell cats are black and brown, with the colors swirled together. While Fudge and Brownie had the darker tortoiseshell coloration, Mini was a dilute torti, meaning the black and brown were muted and looked more like gray and orange.

The three pretty tortoiseshell kittens were found by a runner when they were about six weeks old. A friend of the runner took them in, named them and started the process of taming the feral kittens. Fudge had cuterebra, the parasitic slug, and Brownie a head tilt, so the resident took them to the vet. With the mounting veterinarian bills, I was asked if I could take in the kittens.

The kittens were treated for parasites and the head tilt was either a defect or old injury, but Brownie wasn't in any pain.

All three kittens found good homes, but Mini hit the Jackpot.

My brother-in-law suffered from Huntington's Disease and lived in a care facility. The resident cat in the facility, Molly, had passed away some months before and the residents were asking when they would have a new cat. My sister and her family were fostering the three tortoiseshell kittens and they thought Mini would be a perfect fit for the facility. Mini was very friendly, outgoing and laid back.

Mini, the dilute tortoiseshell moved to the care facility after she was spayed and a little older. The residents had the opportunity to select a name for the kitten and the name my brother-in-law submitted was "Clarissa".

Kitten Clarissa now lives on the third floor of the care facility and has dozens of humans and hands to provide her attention and love. Not bad for a feral kitten.

Marathon

Many rescue facilities in the area are comfortable with taking in pregnant or momma cats with kittens, unless the momma cat happens to be feral. Then I usually get the call. The majority of momma cats with kittens I had interacted with were feral, so having a hissing, spitting momma cat try to get at me while I'm taking her kittens away for some socialization time no longer fazes me.

I picked up the feral momma cat and her six kittens at a local impound. The note on her crate said momma cat would try to escape and run. Luckily, I was able to cover her with a net, get the kittens out, then net her completely, so no running that day. I decided to call her Marathon and she was a gray tabby and all her six kittens were gray tabby or solid gray.

Momma Marathon was a lunger, meaning she would come at me with fangs and claws, so I encouraged her to a higher level in the condo crate with a net before trying to handle the kittens. The six kittens were very hissy and spitty at first, but no bites. The longer I sat in front of the crate and the more curious they became and moved to the front of the crate. They looked about four weeks old, so I thought I would try moist food to see if they would eat. At first, they just chewed on the edge of the plastic bowl, then two of them did try a little food. It looked like there were three males and three females.

One morning Marathon whapped me in the head. While cleaning out the condo crate, I was usually good about staying out of claw reach as she sat on a shelf inside. That morning one of the kittens went back into the crate when I was cleaning it, so I reached inside to get the kitten out and I wasn't paying attention to Marathon like I usually did. She got her arm outside the bars of the crate and got me in the head, but luckily she got my thick hair and my scalp was spared.

The kittens were adorable and fun to watch as they became more mobile and steadier on their feet. The kittens all found forever homes and Momma Marathon was released to a feral cat colony after her spay.

Calais and Tchibi
More orphan kittens

I picked up two, one-week-old orphan kittens from a local impound knowing I had a pregnant female, Palette, already lactating so I was hoping she would accept the kittens. Palette refused the kittens by hissing at them and walking away. Maybe I could slip them in once her kittens were born? I was hoping Palette's kittens would be born soon, because it meant bottle feeding the orphan kittens every two hours, including overnight. I decided I couldn't refer to them as Calico and Tortoiseshell forever, so I named them. The calico became Calais (Greek) means Changing Color and the tortoiseshell was Tchibi (Japanese) means tiny or midget.

They had very healthy appetites and I was glad there were only two of them. They had been going two-and-a-half hours between feedings, but I had one marathon of hourly feedings for three hours straight. They could sure pack it away . I don't really mind bottle feeding; it is the potty part I don't enjoy or the lack of sleep! Newborn kittens need their mother to stimulate them to pass waste, so I had to cover that task. One night, the pair of orphan kittens let me sleep three hours straight. What good kitties! Of course I woke up in a panic when I noticed the time, fearing the kittens had passed away.

When I first got them home, Tchibi was 4.1 ounces and Calais was 4 ounces, but before the kittens were transferred to a lactating queen, (a female cat nursing kittens) Calais had caught up to her littermate in weight and they both weighed in at 4.7 ounces each.

Palette

I picked up pregnant Cherry from a local impound facility and with her beautiful calico markings, I promptly changed her name to Palette. I scheduled an appointment for her at the veterinarian for a checkup to see how close she was to delivering her kittens. She tolerated a nail trim which was good because she had very long, curved nails. Palette was very sweet, and I'm partial to Calicos, so I anticipated that could be a problem when it came time to find her a forever home.

The vet thought Palette would deliver within a week. That night when I checked on Palette she was dripping a bit of milk, but she was also very interested in food, so with those conflictions, I wasn't sure what to think. Generally, pregnant cats don't eat the day or two before delivery.

Palette was really getting to be a wide load. She ate her moist food with gusto again so I figured probably no kittens in the next 24 to 48 hours, but I wanted her to prove me wrong as I was currently bottle feeding the orphan kittens, Calais and Tchibi.

Finally, Palette had her kittens one night. I had checked on her around eight o'clock and all was normal. I checked on her two hours later and she had four kittens. I thought she was done, but when I checked on her the next morning, there were five total.

I decided to let Palette have 48 hours with her kittens before introducing the two orphans. I was still planning on helping Palette out by bottle feeding the orphans, but it would be great if she could just help keep them warm and clean.

It was time for the introduction. I had just fed Palette her second can of cat food for the day (she had dry kitten food available at all times), and I rubbed a bit of moist food on the heads of both Calais and Tchibi. I then put them in with Palette's kittens and mixed them up a bit so everyone shared scents. After Palette was done eating, she jumped into the box with the kittens. She started licking Calais's head right away. Then she smelled Tchibi's bottom and looked up at me with a look that said, "Hey, wait a minute. What are you trying to pull here?" Then she licked Tchibi's head and all was well. I checked on the new arrangement every hour for the next few hours to make sure everyone was adjusting well.

The blended family continued to do well. Palette was an attentive mom and I was happy to get a full eight hours of uninterrupted sleep for the first time in almost a week.

I'm used to having feral momma cats, so having a friendly one was such a joy. I got to interact with the kittens without having to dodge a crabby momma cat's teeth and claws.

When the kittens were older and mobile, I moved Palette and her kittens from the downstairs bathroom to a multi-level condo crate in the kitten playroom. Of course, Tchibi and Calais were much more mobile being about a week older, but everyone was on the move. This means doing headcounts to make sure everyone is accounted for, so I counted from one to seven constantly! At about three weeks old, orphan kitten Tchibi, even attempted to climb the cat tower. She only got about an inch off the floor, but great progress for a kitten her age.

As the kittens became more stable on their feet and more mobile I think Palette was becoming concerned about their activity level. Whenever I would check on her and the kittens, she had moved them from the cat bed into the litter box, and it was too high for them to get out on their own.

The shenanigans during one kitten playtime included Calais climbing up to the first level of the cat tower (about nine inches). Of course I didn't have the camera handy. Then Tchibi and I had our first discussion about not biting fingers. Later, Tchibi and I had our second discussion about not biting fingers. She may have been little, but she made up for it in spunk. When it was time for everyone to go back into the condo crate, Momma Palette was missing in action. I put the kittens into the crate and shut the door, but I didn't latch it. I found Palette under a craft table and when I carried her back into the kitten area, the kittens had busted out. I had to round everybody up again. It was like herding cats!

Kittens usually start on solid food when they are about four weeks old. When I let the kittens out one morning, Azure kept following his mom around meowing so I thought he was probably hungry. It was still a few days before the kittens were four weeks old, but on his next meow I put a little of the moist food I had just set out for Palette on his tongue. He looked confused at first, moved his tongue in and out a bit, then came running at me for more. Of course he ended up wearing most of what he was trying to eat. As all the kittens finally start on moist food, some wore a lot of it, like Magenta, but Narang was the only one who almost sat in the bowl while he eats.

Azure was also the first one to introduce himself to Qwincy. I usually don't let Qwincy play with the kittens until they are six weeks old so they are steadier on their feet. One night, Azure initiated contact with Qwincy, touching noses through the baby gate.

Another night, I came downstairs to some rather dirty kittens. I wasn't sure why Palette wasn't cleaning them. Then, she didn't want anyone nursing from her either. She ate well and still looked good, so I wasn't sure what the issue was. I had never had that happen before. I contacted the vet and wondered whether Palette had decided she was s done nursing, or if something was wrong. The kittens tried to nurse from her, but she wasn't having any of it, so they just ate the moist food I put out. I gave them wash cloth baths to start and then real baths later when they needed it. I guess Palette didn't think I bathed the kittens well enough, because she decided to clean them afterwards and nurse them. It was a complete turnaround from earlier. I was confused.

Then the next morning, there were dirty kittens again. I gave them baths again but Palette critiqued my work and cleaned everyone again. I think she just liked to keep me guessing.

As the kittens got used to being out of the crate running around the play area, when I opened the crate door it made me think of the opening gates at a horse race. I would just open the door and stand back waiting for the stampede of seven kittens and one adult crashing the gate.

I was so exhausted when I got home from work one night, and when I let Palette and the kittens out to play, I just laid on the floor and let them play on and around me. I was on my side and Azure was walking around on top of me and he kept trying to crawl into the pocket of my shorts. The pocket wasn't very big and he could get his head in, but not the rest of his body. He made me laugh for quite some time because he was very persistent in trying to get into the pocket.

Everyone was adopted, but Cyan (now named Finley) was adopted by a coworker, so I still receive updates on him and his antics.

The Great Escape

We were participating in a TNR spay/neuter event in a neighborhood and had trapped about 50 feral cats that were housed in a machine shed overnight to be sterilized on a mobile unit the next day. One of the volunteers was bringing in a trapped gray tabby cat, she tripped and fell, and when the trap fell, the cat got loose in the shed. We reset the trap to hopefully get the cat overnight. However, the next day, the trap was empty. We set it again that night after the spay/neuter event, and the next morning, we had the cat again. Because the mobile unit had done all the surgeries the day before, I offered to take the cat home and keep him until I could get him to another of the mobile clinics.

The Great Escape Cat Plays Crocodile

When I went to feed The Great Escape Cat the next morning, it had trashed the crate overnight, so all I saw was shredded newspaper. As I approached the crate, I could see one large yellow eye looking out from the shredded newspaper, and it reminded me of a crocodile in the water with just the eyes showing. The explosion that followed when I opened the crate was like a crocodile coming out of the water. It was tough, but I was able to swap out the litter box and put in food and fresh water without the cat getting away again.

The Great Escape Cat was neutered at the next mobile clinic and released back to his home territory.

Wrigley
Little Kitten Lost

I keep trying to stick to our new focus; no more trapping and just maintaining the feral cat colonies that I have already trapped. However, the calls about feral mommas and their babies just break my heart. I was called about trapping a feral momma with a litter of three-day-old kittens in a neighboring town.

The momma cat had her kittens under a bay window. I set the trap by the window, but we didn't get momma cat. The next day we tried again, but she had moved her kittens. I was looking around the large yard to see if I could find where she moved them, but without any luck. Then I heard a faint mewing sound. It looked like she dropped one of the kittens while she was moving them. I found the kitten under a tree, but we couldn't find where she took the others.

I put the kitten under my shirt to stay warm and took him home. The kitten was white with gray markings, including a gray triangle strategically placed over his nose. I named him Wrigley for the way the kitten's ears wiggled while it nursed from the bottle. I wasn't sure how long the kitten had been alone under the tree so I hoped it could hold on until we found a lactating queen. The most important things for a newborn kitten are warmth and milk, both of which he had been without for an undetermined amount of time.

Wrigley made it through the first night, waking up every two hours to eat. I wasn't sure of the gender, but I used he as the pronoun. He was a slow nurser and he would fall asleep while nursing. Not a problem for a momma cat, but difficult for a tired human who just wants to go back to sleep. I had to keep waking him up while he was feeding to make sure he got enough so I could sleep another two hours.

I made a little pocket out of a wash cloth and sewed a ribbon to it so I could wear it around my neck. I put Wrigley into the little sling and wore him under my shirt to keep him warm. While I had bottle fed many kittens before, this was the first time it was a solo kitten that didn't have a littermate to help keep him warm.

Even though he was doing well with bottle feeding, I was actively looking for a lactating queen for Little Wrigley. It was his best chance of survival and my best chance of getting some much needed beauty sleep. Finally, after networking via facebook and email, Wrigley had a new surrogate momma cat. Wrigley was accepted by the momma cat and he was busy nursing while she cleaned him when I left the residence. Along with the momma cat, he also had four three-week-old kittens to help keep him warm!

As for me, I slept ten hours straight the night Wrigley went to his new home. I took Qwincy out

127

to do his business, and then I slept for another two hours.

Wrigley thrived with his new feline family and found a forever home.

Stitch and Knit
Two Pregnant Females...Not

I can never say no to pregnant feral cats.

Along with several other cats, Stitch and Knit were abandoned in a trailer home after the family moved away in the night. Most of the cats were taken in by animal control, but a kind resident took in these pregnant ladies and spent three weeks trying to find an agency that would take them. I agreed to take them and the good Samaritan brought the cats to my house. Stitch's stomach was about twice the size of Knit's so I was expecting kittens soon.

I couldn't figure out why my house smelled like an unneutered male cat for the next two days, so I did a gender check on the two pregnant ferals. The bigger cat, Stitch, was actually a chunky male. The smaller cat, Knit, was a female. They were attached to each other so I hated to separate them, but I keep all the smelly boys in the garage. I thought if the female hadn't been pregnant when initially trapped, she more than likely was pregnant now.

I took the female to the veterinarian to be x-rayed and she actually wasn't pregnant. They were just two chunky cats. They were both vetted and sterilized and released into a colony.

Mr. Cranky Pants

I didn't want to take the kitten.

We were participating in another TNR spay/neuter event and one of the volunteers obtained two sick kittens from one of the residents. The kittens were anemic from being covered in fleas. The smaller of the two was very listless and dehydrated. The volunteer soon became overwhelmed with the prospect of caring for the two kittens.

An event supporter took the smaller and sicker of the two kittens and then asked if I would take the other kitten. I declined because I already had enough on my plate with the feral cats I had at home. Over the course of the day however, the volunteer went on and on about her concerns of being able to take care of the kitten and I finally relented and said I would take the kitten. He was in a crate at the event and every time we got near him, he would hiss and spit at us, so I called him Mr. Cranky Pants. We had to net him just to get flea preventative on him.

It is much easier taming feral kittens when they are on their own since they have no littermate to bond with so the human is the next best thing. Mr. Cranky Pants tamed rather quickly and became quite the snuggler and purrer. A few times I thought about keeping him, but then he would do something like climb the curtains or walk across the entertainment center and I would remember how much work kittens are and I would remain content with my older, earth bound cats.

However, I had a setback with Mr. Cranky Pants when I was getting him ready to go to the adoption event. The night before when I was picking him up to put him in the crate at bedtime, Qwincy started barking, Mr. C got startled, jumped out of my hand and went into hiding. I pulled out the treats, called "Treat, Treat!" and Mr. Cranky Pants came out to go into his crate for a treat. The next morning when I went to his crate, Mr. Cranky Pants started hissing and when I reached in to take him out, he bit me, so it looked like we would have to start taming all over again.

When I arrived home from running all my errands and taking Qwincy to the dog park later that day, Mr. C was back to normal! I went to his crate and he hissed at me, but when I opened the crate and touched him, he immediately started purring. I decided to take his hissing and biting that morning as a sign that he was supposed to stay with me for some reason, curtain climbing and all.

Even though he is now a sweet, loving cat, I kept his name as Mr. Cranky Pants. He and cat Klondike are the best of friends and where you see one, the other is right there as well. Mr. C sits on my lap whenever I'm on the couch and curls up next to me at night. Now, I can't imagine life without the kitten I didn't want.

Clarissa Wolf is originally from Bismarck, ND and currently lives in Chaska, MN with Qwincy and several cats.

Since closing her nonprofit Spay the Strays, Fix the Ferals at the end of 2012, Clarissa has been practicing Trap Neuter Return and taming feral kittens with several different Minnesota rescues.

Clarissa has also written three children's books about feral cats:

Qwincy, Feral Kitten Tamer, Cat Cat Feral Cat and *Orange Fizz.*

When not feigning the claws and teeth of feral cats, Clarissa loves Zumba, enjoys reading mysteries and biographies, doing ceramics and walking with Qwincy.

CPSIA information can be obtained at www.ICGtesting.com
Printed in the USA
BVOW02s0322071013

333059BV00001B/2/P

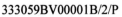

9 781612 861005